The Great Tours: Greece and Turkey, from Athens to Istanbul

John R. Hale, Ph.D.

THE
GREAT
COURSES®

PUBLISHED BY:

THE GREAT COURSES
Corporate Headquarters
4840 Westfields Boulevard, Suite 500
Chantilly, Virginia 20151-2299
Phone: 1-800-832-2412
Fax: 703-378-3819
www.thegreatcourses.com

Copyright © The Teaching Company, 2011

Printed in the United States of America

This book is in copyright. All rights reserved.

Without limiting the rights under copyright reserved above,
no part of this publication may be reproduced, stored in
or introduced into a retrieval system, or transmitted,
in any form, or by any means
(electronic, mechanical, photocopying, recording, or otherwise),
without the prior written permission of
The Teaching Company.

John R. Hale, Ph.D.
Director of Liberal Studies
University of Louisville

Professor John R. Hale, Director of Liberal Studies at the University of Louisville, is an archaeologist with fieldwork and research experience at sites in Greece, Turkey, England, Scandinavia, Portugal, Italy, Jordan, Guatemala, and the Ohio River Valley. Archaeology has been the focus of Professor Hale's career, and he has led student and adult tours to many of the sites he has worked on or studied, especially in Greece and Turkey. At the University of Louisville, Professor Hale teaches introductory courses on archaeology and specialized courses on the Bronze Age, the ancient Greeks, the Roman world, Celtic cultures, Vikings, and nautical and underwater archaeology.

During more than 30 years of archaeological work, Professor Hale has excavated at a Romano-British town in Lincolnshire, England, as well as at a Roman villa in Portugal; has carried out interdisciplinary studies of ancient oracle sites in Greece and Turkey, including the famed Delphic oracle; and has participated in an undersea search in Greek waters for lost fleets from the Greek and Persian wars. In addition, Professor Hale is a member of a scientific team developing and refining a method for dating mortar, concrete, and plaster from ancient buildings—a method that employs radiocarbon analysis with an accelerator mass spectrometer.

Professor Hale completed his undergraduate studies at Yale and received his Ph.D. from the University of Cambridge. The subject of his dissertation was the Bronze Age ancestry of the Viking longship, a study that involved field surveys of ship designs in prehistoric rock art in southern Norway and Sweden. His work has been published in *Scientific American, Antiquity, Journal of Roman Archaeology*, and *The Classical Bulletin*. Most of Professor Hale's work is interdisciplinary and involves collaborations with geologists, chemists, nuclear physicists, historians, zoologists, botanists, physical anthropologists, geographers, and art historians. His most recent book is *Lords of the Sea: The Epic Story of the Athenian Navy and the Birth of Democracy*, published in 2009.

As a national lecturer for the Archaeological Institute of America, Professor Hale presents lectures in many cities throughout the United States and Canada, and he has also made lecture tours to South Africa, Finland, Australia, and New Zealand. He has received numerous awards for his distinguished teaching, including the Panhellenic Teacher of the Year Award and the Delphi Center Award.

Professor Hale is the instructor of four other Great Courses: *Exploring the Roots of Religion, The Greek and Persian Wars, Classical Archaeology of Ancient Greece and Rome*, and *The Art of Public Speaking: Lessons from the Greatest Speeches in History.* ∎

Table of Contents

INTRODUCTION

Professor Biography i
Course Scope 1

LECTURE GUIDES

LECTURE 1
Touring the Cradle of Western Civilization 3

LECTURE 2
Athens—Around the Acropolis and Parthenon 9

LECTURE 3
In the Footsteps of Socrates—Historic Athens 15

LECTURE 4
Around Attica—Temples and Mysteries 22

LECTURE 5
Seeking the Good Life—Corinth to Epidauros 27

LECTURE 6
Mycenae—Where Kings Planned the Trojan War 31

LECTURE 7
Around Nafplio—Greek History at a Glance 37

LECTURE 8
Ancient Olympia—Gods, Games, and Temples 43

LECTURE 9
Quest for Wisdom at Apollo's Oracle—Delphi 48

Table of Contents

LECTURE 10
Byzantine Outposts—Monemvasia and Mistra....................55

LECTURE 11
Cruising the Islands—Mykonos and Delos.........................61

LECTURE 12
Aegean Ring of Fire—Milos and Santorini 66

LECTURE 13
Exploring Crete—Realm of Ancient Minoans 71

LECTURE 14
Lure of the Labyrinth—Palace at Knossos 78

LECTURE 15
The Dodecanese—Kos, Patmos, and Rhodes....................83

LECTURE 16
Welcome to Turkey—The Turquoise Coast........................90

LECTURE 17
Central Turkey—Ankara, Konya, Cappadocia....................96

LECTURE 18
Up the Meander River—Priene to Pamukkale...................102

LECTURE 19
A Wonder of the World—Ephesus.................................109

LECTURE 20
Royal Cities of Asia—Pergamon and Sardis 116

LECTURE 21
Troy—Beyond Homer and the Trojan Horse 123

LECTURE 22
Istanbul—Capital of the Byzantine Emperors...................129

Table of Contents

LECTURE 23
The Pearl of Constantinople—Hagia Sophia 135

LECTURE 24
Ottoman Istanbul—Mosques, Palaces, Bazaars 140

SUPPLEMENTAL MATERIAL

Map of Athens and the Acropolis 147
Map of Istanbul 148
Embassy Contact Information 149
Contact Information for Major Sites 151
Bibliography 152

The Great Tours:
Greece and Turkey, from Athens to Istanbul

Scope:

To travel the Aegean is to travel through the history of Western civilization. The poetry of Homer was composed along these shores; here Hippocrates made the West's first systematic medical observations, and the free men of Athens set out to govern themselves. Great empire builders like the Minoans, the Hittites, the Myceneans, the Macedonian Greeks, the Romans, and the Ottoman Turks all left their mark on these landscapes and on the entire world from their bases of power here in the eastern Mediterranean.

But why visit? Well, for one thing, the Aegean is one of the most beautiful places in the world. This land where three continents collide offers gorgeous volcanic-sand beaches, dramatic landscapes, and crystal-clear waters enough to satisfy any seeker of paradise, not to mention fine food and wine. But it also offers the traveler a unique opportunity to interact with history. This course will take you to sites where you can share in local life as it has been lived in the Aegean for hundreds, even thousands of years. But more than that, almost everywhere you look, you will find archaeological wonders—some mysterious, some well understood—just waiting to be explored. In fact, the Aegean has preserved more of its history than perhaps any other place on earth.

This course uses the two great cities of Athens and Istanbul as bookends for a journey around the Aegean. Athens was the great intellectual center of ancient Greece, as well as the center of a mighty military league and the birthplace of democratic government. Istanbul, at the crossroads of Europe and Asia, has long been the border of East and West, the place where cultures have met, both in conflict and in harmony, and shows its proudly complex heritage in every street and stone. Through several lectures on each, you will visit famous sites such as Athens's Acropolis and Istanbul's Hagia Sophia, as well as lesser-known gems like the archaeological museums hidden in Athens's metro system and the Great Palace Mosaic in Istanbul. But these cities are not the limits of our explorations.

The Aegean is the geologic meeting place of three continents—Europe, Asia, and Africa. That collision drove up dozens of islands with fascinating volcanic and seismic stories to tell. From hot springs and gorges to calderas and cliffs of obsidian, the Aegean islands offer landscapes to dazzle the eyes. Each of these islands also has much to offer the curious historian and amateur archaeologist, from the mysteries of the Minoan palace builders of Crete to the drowned cities off the islands' coasts, which you can explore by boat and snorkel. Meanwhile, in the interior of the land once known as Anatolia or Asia Minor (now called Turkey), you can visit catacombs belonging to the oldest Christian worshipers, the many successive cities of Troy, or a Neolithic "tell" where the people buried their dead inside their homes and prayed to the mother goddess we know only as the mistress of beasts.

Many ghosts will rise out of the past to join us on our trip—Hector and Achilles, Alexander and Xerxes, Saint Paul the Apostle and Saint John the Divine, Crusader armies and Ottoman Janissaries. Each of them is a part of the wonderful mosaic that make the Aegean a must-see destination for any lover of history. ■

Touring the Cradle of Western Civilization
Lecture 1

Welcome to the extraordinary world of the Aegean. In my work as an archaeologist, my Mediterranean journeys involve visiting the temples of the oracles and studying the geology beneath them. I wade into chest-high water to explore flooded sites, and I get even wetter searching for shipwrecks. It is my pleasure to share with you my discoveries and the discoveries of hundreds of archaeologists, researchers, and historians who have gone before me. I hope these lectures will enable you to catch a glimpse of the colorful and exciting Aegean world that once was.

- Whether you are planning your first trip, have visited many times and are looking for new insights, or are simply an armchair traveler, there could not be a more wonderful spot on earth to explore than the Aegean.

- The plan is to travel in stages with one or two sites at each stage. You will visit great cities like Athens or Ephesus and small sites out in the countryside. You want to get the whole length and breadth of this ancient world, the stage on which the drama of Western civilization was played out.

- The Aegean Sea is a uniquely beautiful place. Cold, clear mountain air comes down out of the mountains of Thrace—modern Bulgaria. The waters are dazzlingly clear as well; you can sometimes see 100 feet down to reefs and shipwrecks.

- Added to this beauty is the sheer geological interest of the region. This is a spot where three continents collide—Europe, Asia, and Africa—pushing up mountains like Parnassus and Olympus, sinking whole cities and creating sites that recall the legend of Atlantis.

3

- You will meet an incredible cast of characters. Myths have attached themselves to the landscape at almost every site visited. You will get to know poets like Homer who put those myths into verse, and you will meet the great philosophers who made Athens the intellectual center of the world that, in some ways, has never been surpassed.

- Medicine was also founded in this corner of the world, and we will visit sites like Epidauros with sanctuaries to the Greek god of medicine, Aesculapius. We will visit Pergamon in Turkey, where the famous ancient physician and writer Galen trained and practiced his art. We will also visit the island of Kos, the home of Hippocrates, for whom the Hippocratic oath is named.

- The ancient Mediterranean peoples loved entertainment, and some of the biggest ruins are their stadiums and their open-air theaters—some the latter with near-perfect acoustics, a marvel of ancient engineering.

- This ancient world is the forerunner of the Western world, and I hope that when we have finished our journey you will feel much closer to these people. You will feel that their lives in some way have shaped your own and that their spirit is living on in our own time.

- During my own travels through this cradle of Western civilization, stereotypes I had nursed through my younger days were shattered. I was brought up to believe that the Greeks only built in white marble. Nothing could be further from the truth; their buildings and art were garish, bright, and dazzling. This course will try to bring back these colors, to help you put on magic glasses to see what has been lost to time.

- These lectures will give you many more surprises, like the world's oldest analog computer—now at the National Museum in Athens—dating to about 100 B.C. This little contraption served as a planetarium, showing the relationships of all the heavenly bodies, even predicting eclipses 2,000 years before such a thing was heard of in our modern world.

- Sardis, on the western coast of Turkey, is the place where money was invented. Silver and gold from the nearby hills flow down to the city by river, where it was panned and minted by the Lydians. Sardis is also home to the most extraordinary surviving Jewish synagogue from the ancient world.

- Istanbul is home to one of the great buildings of the world, Hagia Sophia ("Holy Wisdom"), built by Emperor Justinian as a Christian church and later, under the Ottomans, converted to a mosque. Here we see a remarkable collision of cultures, a fusing of Christianity and Islam and, perhaps most surprisingly, graffiti that hints of a Viking presence in the ancient Byzantine world.

Hagia Sophia, one of the most famous buildings in the world, is one of many jewels you will discover in the great city of Istanbul.

5

- You will also see the grim side of cultures meeting, colliding, fusing, and learning from each other throughout the Mediterranean world. The Trojan War was just an overture to a history riddled with conflict and conquest; one of the fundamental fault lines in human history runs right down the middle of the Aegean Sea—Asia on one side, Europe on the other. This is where the concept of East versus West was born.

- We cannot ignore, as we look at these fantastic sights, the forces of creativity that brought them into being, nor the forces of conflict and destruction that left them in ruins. There are lessons to be learned here.

- The ancient world gave prominence to the idea that there is nothing more powerful than the human will. You will meet some real giants in the ancient Aegean, people who would affect human history to this day and beyond: Cleisthenes, founder of democracy; Alexander the Great, the conqueror who dreamed of fusing East and West; the Apostle Paul, who put Christianity on the path from obscure Jewish sect to worldwide religion; and many more.

- To start our journey on the right foot, I'd like to introduce you to some ancient travelers' recommendations for traveling the Aegean:

    o Wear a hat. That fine clear air offers no buffer between you and the sun. You can be hit with sunstroke almost before you know it. Think of Hermes, the Greek god of travel and the only god who always wears a hat.

    o Always have plenty of water with you. Every ancient traveler carried an animal-skin flask, drinking from it regularly and refilling it at every spring they passed.

    o If you have the choice, travel by boat, not by land. In the ancient world, Greece had no good roads until the Romans came; everyone traveled by sea. You do not need an expensive cruise ship. Look for ferries and water buses.

- Take a book wherever you go. A comedy by the Athenian playwright Aristophanes from the late 5th century B.C. tells us that even the god Dionysus—the god of wine—takes along some reading to pass the time on board these ships. Try reading something as a counterpoint to your own adventures—Homer's *Odyssey* or Orhan Mamuk's *Istanbul, Memories of a City*.

- Do not visit the Aegean in the winter. While it is extraordinary to see these ruins in the snow, many sites shut down in the winter. The sea lanes close. Save your trip for spring, summer, or fall—especially spring.

- Try to take the middle of the day off. The ancients ducked inside when the sun got high. They'd have a nice long, leisurely lunch and a postlunch nap. The best time to visit the ruins is the late afternoon, when the crowds thin and the light turns golden.

- Keep track of the phases of the moon. Full moons in good weather were marked out for great festivals in the ancient Aegean. It is still an extraordinary experience to sit on a rooftop and see the full moon rising over the Parthenon or from the deck of an excursion ship in the Bosporus at Istanbul.

- Take the plunge and buy some reproductions. Ancient travelers loved them. In many cases, we do not have original art works from the ancient world. We have to thank the tourist industry of 2,000 years ago for creating replicas.

- Seek out the spas and baths of the ancient world on both sides of the Aegean, like those at Thermopylae that helped the Spartans hold Xerxes and the Persians at bay for three days. And the mud baths at Kaunos on the Turquoise Coast of southwestern Turkey.

○ Eat and drink as the locals eat and drink. You are there to experience their world, and they know the best wine, bread, fruit, vegetables, and meat produced in their world, along with the best concoctions made from them.

○ Finally, keep a journal and write in it every day. The ancients did. We have records from the travels of Solon, Herodotus, and Pausanias—author of the world's first travel guidebook. Never think that people will not be interested. Your insights may be new, and your record may be a lasting testament that opens up this world to a new generation of readers.

Daypack Essentials

When you head out for a day of touring in the Aegean region, always bring a bag that contains these items:

- sun hat and sunblock

- bottled water

- camera

- a book to read and a book to write in (don't forget a pen!)

- maps, brochures, and tour books

- local currency, credit cards or travelers' checks, and identification

- a cell phone and emergency contact information list (See the appendix for embassy and other emergency contact numbers.)

- space to hold your souvenirs.

Athens—Around the Acropolis and Parthenon
Lecture 2

Athens is the capital of the modern nation of Greece, and in terms of its contributions to art, architecture, philosophy, history, and culture overall, it was the true heart of the golden age of classical Greece. Its chief landmark is the Acropolis, meaning "high city." The Acropolis is the symbol of Athens, and the Parthenon that crowns it is the emblem of classical civilization.

- The stone stairs that greet you beyond the Acropolis's entrance gate are a set of marble steps that, over two millennia ago, the entire population of Athens would climb in procession on the first day of Hekatombaion (roughly our July) each year. At the top, they would sacrifice 100 oxen to Athena, the goddess of wisdom and of Athens itself. (In those days, a ramp ran parallel to the steps for the oxen.)

- Be careful on these steps and the site itself; the Acropolis is a mass of very resistant limestone and marble. There are places on the Acropolis, steps included, that are as slippery as a skating rink.

- As you look up from the base of the steps, to your right is a great stone bastion topped by a delicate little temple to the goddess Athena Nike—Athena in her guise as goddess of victory. Victory itself is always shown as a figure with wings, usually carrying a laurel wreath to put on the victor's head and blowing a trumpet to announce the victory. This temple was erected to thank the goddess for a battle won in the 420s B.C.

- Looking straight up the stairs, you will see a grand gatehouse called the propylaea ("front gates"). These hide from sight the Mycenaean palace gates from about 1,000 years before the time of Pericles and the classical Greeks of the 5th century B.C. who put up the propylaeum and the Parthenon.

- The Acropolis was originally the site of a Mycenaean king's palace, a man who ruled Attica as a vassal to Agamemnon. This Bronze Age king brought worship of Athena to the site. In building the Parthenon, the classical Athenians wiped out almost every trace of the Mycenaean palace.

- The Athenians prized the propylaea more than almost any other building they had created. Most people did not go up to the top of the rock on a regular basis. It was a place for the priests and priestesses. It is funny that we so prize the Parthenon when the ancient Athenians did not.

- In that celebration on the first day of Hekatombaion, the procession started in the agora, or marketplace. The chief feature of the parade was a ship on wheels; Athens was a city of the sea. A peplos, or robe, that the young noble girls of the city had spent the year making was drawn through the city mounted on its mast like a sail.

© Comstock/Thinkstock.

The Parthenon is in many ways the ultimate symbol of the city of Athens, yet much of what visitors assume they know about it is incorrect.

- Entering the shade of the propylaea, to your left is the site of one of classical Athens's many art museums. Today, the paintings are gone, and the press of tourists will move you quickly through the site.

- Exiting the propylaea between Doric columns, you will find yourself in an empty courtyard. In the classical era, a 50-foot-high bronze statue of Athena stood here, cast by the great sculptor Phidias. The sun shining on Athena's spear tip and helmet was so dazzling that mariners all the way out at sea could pick it out as a landmark.

- During the late Roman Empire, the statue was removed to adorn the then-new city of Constantinople, but today no one is sure what became of it.

- This empty space was also the site of the original temple of Athena Polias—Athena as goddess of the city. It was destroyed by the armies of Xerxes, king of Persia, who seized the evacuated city in 480 B.C. Xerxes ordered the temple burned because the Athenian army had earlier helped burn a temple to the Persian mother goddess in Sardis.

- When the Athenians returned, they left the remains of the temple as a war monument, and it remained part of the city's Athena cult right through the classical period, down to the end of the 5th century B.C.

- To the right of this space is the Parthenon. Despite all the glory and meaning we attach to it, in some ways it is not what it appears to be.

   o First, you are looking at the back of the temple. The front of the temple is oriented toward the east, but the gate is at the west because the eastern face of the Acropolis was too steep for the steps and ramps.

   o Second, in the classical era this plain white marble was garishly painted in blue, red, and gold. The Greeks thought sculptures should look lifelike. They did not idealize white marble the way we do.

- Walk next along the Parthenon's north colonnade and reflect on the architectural refinements and sleight-of-hand called into play by Phidias and the architects in designing and building this structure. It looks like everything is perfectly straight and rectangular, yet there is scarcely a straight line in this entire building.

- The Greeks realized that straight lines in huge Doric temples gave an impression of heaviness, sagging, and squatness, so every column in the Parthenon swells a little bit in the middle. The stylobate, or base, of the temple curves slightly upward.

- Looking up, you can see fragments of the frieze inside the first set of columns. When you get to the middle of the temple, you will see the terrible damage from an explosion in 1687 when a Venetian mortar shell blew up a store of gunpowder that their enemies, the Turks, had stored here.

- Fortunately, a couple of traveling English artists had sketched some sculptures from the ends of the damaged area just a few years before the explosion. The one to the west showed Athena in contest with Poseidon for the patronage of Athens. The one to the east showed Athena's birth, springing forth from the head of Zeus.

- In a normal temple, the sacrifice of a large group of animals like the 100 oxen would take place in right in front, but the Parthenon is not a normal temple—in fact, it is not a temple at all! It is actually a gigantic war trophy, commemorating the Athenian victories over the Persians down to the 440s B.C.

- The Parthenon is also a glorification of Pericles and his family, the Achaemenids, and it was a treasury for the tribute paid by 150 islands and cities to Athens.

- Inside the Parthenon, the great statue of Athena was not a holy statue. The gold plating on its ivory surface could be pulled off and melted down in times of financial emergency. Although we have

Roman-era reproductions of that statue, all trace of it is now gone except for a little square socket in the floor where it was anchored.

- Chances are you will not be allowed into the shattered Parthenon itself. They have been restoring it for many more decades than it actually took to build.

- Above the eastern door and behind the main columns is the famous Parthenon frieze, which showed the procession leading up to the Acropolis, all the people of Athens celebrating their goddess, and the Olympian gods themselves coming to celebrate Athena's birthday with her. In the middle, a priest takes the peplos and makes ready to offer it to the goddess as a new dress for the new year.

- On the outside, just above the column capitals, you can see clusters of holes along the architrave. Each used to hold a bronze letter, spelling out the message "Alexander, king, dedicates these shields to the goddess on his behalf and on behalf of the Greeks, except for the Spartans." This tribute to Athena by Alexander the Great commemorated his first great victory in Asia.

Beautiful Inside and Out

During the first restoration of the Parthenon, engineers attempted to strengthen the columns by taking the drums apart and replacing the cedar plugs connecting them with iron bars. Years later, it was realized that the iron was rusting, so recently engineers have started replacing the iron bars with titanium ones.

To their surprise, the engineers found an undisturbed column—one that was missed in the first restoration—with its original cedar plug. Although the wood was 2,500 years old, the joint between the column drums was so tight that the cedar still smelled fresh. The talent and precision of the Parthenon's ancient builders was truly remarkable!

- Looking down from the south parapet, you can see the modern building housing the Acropolis Museum. In the museum, you will see the original sculptures from the Parthenon; the ones you see on the building are plaster casts. The acid rainfall of Athens is too brutal on marble to leave these treasures out in the open.

- The museum's lower levels house the oldest antiquities; at the top you will see the fragments that survived the explosion in 1687, including plaster casts of the famous Elgin Marbles. (The originals are, controversially, still in the British Museum.)

- The eastern end of the Acropolis forms a shape something like the prow of a ship. If you stand there and look back toward the propylaea, you can see the delicate, Ionic-style Erechtheum, which housed the real cult statue of Athena—the true temple. The little olive tree growing next to it is, according to legend, a descendent of the one that Athena planted when she claimed Attica for her own.

- The flagpole at the east end of the Acropolis commemorates a hero of the Greek resistance against the Nazis. On a may day in 1941, the Germans entered Athens and ordered a soldier to take down the Greek flag on the Acropolis and replace it with a Third Reich flag. The soldier brought down the flag, wrapped it around himself, and dove from the Acropolis to his death. That story spread and ignited the resistance movement in Greece.

In the Footsteps of Socrates—Historic Athens
Lecture 3

This "walk around the rock" takes us around the base of the Acropolis at the heart of ancient and modern Athens. We start at the east end, below the Acropolis flagpole, on the level of the main city, in a small square whose centerpiece is the Monument of Lysicrates, the world's oldest monument in the Corinthian style.

- Lysicrates was a naval hero and a *choregos*—a sponsor of theatrical shows, what we would today call a producer. He erected this monument in tribute to his chorus's victory in a performance competition.

- Built in the 320s B.C., the monument is one of the must-see spots in Athens, a beautiful circle of Corinthian columns with a frieze above showing the subject of the song that won the contest—the infant Dionysus kidnapped by pirates.

- The square around Lysicrates's Monument is a great place to shop for souvenirs—particularly theatrical masks for stock characters from Athenian plays, the same sort of souvenirs people bought here in antiquity.

- The square is also a focal point for a number of streets running into the old part of Athens, the Plaka, that dominates the north and east sides of the Acropolis.

- From the monument, look down the street called Lysicratu (that is, Lysicrates's street). Beyond the traffic, you can see the Arch of Hadrian. In A.D. 131, the Roman emperor Hadrian, who loved Athens, decided to beautify the city. This arch was the gateway to a whole set of Roman monuments, many now gone, that climaxed with the Temple of Olympian Zeus.

- The temple was started more than 700 years before Hadrian's time, but on too grand a scale; it would have been bigger than the Parthenon. The site languished for centuries until Hadrian decided to complete it not in the original Doric style but in the much newer Corinthian style. About a dozen Corinthian columns, the tallest columns in Athens, still mark the spot.

- It is worth pausing here to think about the fate of so many of classical Athens's great buildings and artworks. Much of the marble was scavenged to make plaster and cement for other building projects in later eras, particularly during the Ottoman Turkish period.

- Next, head south from the square toward the modern Grand Promenade, built as a tourist-friendly city center for the 2004 Summer Olympics but now beloved by the locals, too. This promenade is the walkway for most of our tour around the rock.

- Near the Grand Promenade is a monument to the late Melina Mercouri, a great actress best known to English-speaking audiences for her roles in the two films *Topkapi* and *Never on Sunday*. Mercouri also served as Greece's minister of culture from 1981 to 1989. The chief warrior in the battle to get the Elgin Marbles returned to Greece, Mercuri argued that any artwork that was originally part of an architectural monument belongs with that monument.

- The Grand Promenade is also where we find the Acropolis metro station. Not only is Athens's metro a great transportation network, but the stations are decorated with antiquities that were discovered during the stations' construction. Each one is a miniature museum. Monastiraki and Syntagma Square (Constitution Square) stations are particularly worth visiting for their beautifully preserved Greek and Roman viaducts.

- Continue south along the base of the Acropolis toward the Theater of Dionysus on the south slope. Dionysus was the god of wine and intoxication—of altered states, and every time an actor puts on a mask, that is an altered state.

- The empty semicircular space at the center of the theater is the orchestra, which is not a pit for musicians as we use the word but a dance floor. Ecstatic dance was the heart and soul of every Dionysiac theater.

- Originally there would have been an altar to Dionysus in the middle of the orchestra. On performance days, Dionysus's statue was brought in a procession from his temple to a seat in front of the orchestra so the god could watch the show.

- Although the greatest surviving works of ancient Greek theater were written by Athenians—Aeschylus, Sophocles, Euripides, and Aristophanes—this building was built long after their deaths. In their time, the high classical period of the 5th century B.C., the theater was probably rectangular and much smaller.

- Only the lower portion of the skene, or stage building, from which actors made their entrances and exits remains today. The chorus entered and exited from the side wings, or parodoi. For many people, the chorus was the main attraction of the ancient theater, with its songs, dances, and glorious, flamboyant costumes, like the chorus of a Broadway musical today.

- The next stop south along the Grand Promenade is the Odeon of Herodes Atticus, a towering facade of Roman arches and vaults. This grand space, built in A.D. 160 with 34 tiers of seats, was not a theater for plays but for music and recitations. The site has wonderful acoustics and still hosts summer music festivals today.

- This site raises a question for archaeologists. Most odeons were roofed with cedar, but many people speculate that this space was too large and its stage building too tall for the engineers of Herodes Atticus's day. If it was roofed, it makes the site even more extraordinary.

- Continuing around the western end of the Acropolis, near the steps to the propylaea, we find the Hill of the Monument of Philopappus on our left. These rarely visited sites put you almost on eye-level with the Parthenon and are great spots to take photos.

- To see the beginnings of democratic government in Athens, ascend the nearby hill called the Pnyx ("the place of the crowd"). This is where the assembly of democratic Athens met. You can see, although not stand on, the bema—the speakers' platform from which Pericles and his successors addressed the crowds. There's another great view of the Acropolis from here as well.

- The Areopagus Rock ("Hill of Ares") is a rare kind of site— a temple to the god of war. The ancient Greeks, warlike though they were, did not make much of his cult. The Areopagus is also where the Apostle Paul was questioned by the Council of the Aeropagus, an assembly of aristocrats that usually opposed the democratic assembly. The Areopagus tends to be extremely slippery; walk cautiously.

- Continue downhill along the Grand Promenade, on your left are many cafés with rooftop seating, fantastic views, and great authentic Athenian food.

- At the bottom of the hill is the old potter's quarter of Athens, the Kerameikos. Pottery made Athens rich, thanks to the fine clay that the Eridanos and other sluggish rivers brought down from the surrounding hills. In Mycenaean times, this was also the public burial grounds of Athens.

Doric, Ionic, Corinthian:
A Primer

Ancient Greek architecture is divided into three orders, or styles, most easily distinguished by the decoration of the capitals—the tops—of a building's columns.

- Doric columns are simple and austere, just a stack of smooth, flatish blocks.

- Ionic columns are topped by distinctive scrolls, sometimes called volutes.

- Corinthian columns are the most elaborate, decorated with both scrollwork and stylized leaves.

All three styles were later adopted by Roman architects and can be seen in later buildings constructed throughout the world, from the medieval cathedrals of Europe to the modern government buildings of Washington DC.

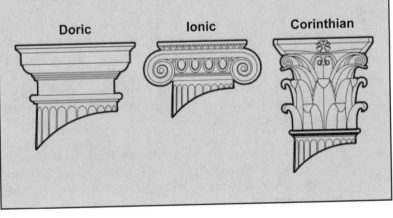

| Doric | Ionic | Corinthian |

© iStockphoto/Thinkstock.

- From the Kerameikos the Dipylon, a gigantic double gate, marks the start of the sacred way that led out to Plato's Academy. Athena's birthday parade also began here. The nearby Archaeological Museum of Kerameikos contains many dazzling tomb sculptures.

- Ahead lies the agora, the market of classical Athens. It was a civic center, a political center, a market, and a gathering place for Athens's citizens. The view to our left is dominated by the reconstruction of the Stoa of Attalos II. Straight ahead are columns topped by white marble giants. They were gifts from Agrippa, friend and son-in-law of Emperor Augustus. Agrippa intended the statues to be part of the facade of an odeon.

- The agora was hit hard by time. Most of the upper structures of its buildings were taken away for plaster making. The exception is on the right on a little hill—the most intact Doric temple in all of Greece, dedicated to Hephaestos, god of smiths and metalworkers. In the 7th century A.D., this temple was turned into the Church of Saint George (he of the dragon), so it was mostly preserved, although much of its pagan statuary had its defining features knocked off.

- At the southeast corner as you stand facing the main door, a statue of the Minotaur of the Theseus myth remains intact. So does the temple cella, the central room of the temple that held the statue of the god, along with a statue of Athena. Outside, archaeologists have found evidence that there were once colonnades of shrubs or trees extending the colonnades of the temple in one of the world's oldest examples of landscape architecture.

- Fragments of buildings remain in the agora. This is where Socrates used to walk—strolling, arguing, and learning from craftsmen, including Simon the cobbler, whose actual house and workshop may have been found.

- Next, return to the Stoa of Attalos II. Reconstructed in the mid-20th century with funds from John D. Rockefeller, the original building was a gift from the king of Asia Minor to the Athenians in the 2nd century B.C. Today, it is a museum of Athenian democracy, holding treasures from both the political sphere and ordinary Athenian life.

- Before ending your tour, take one look back at the east end of the Acropolis and look for caves carved into the rock. One is called the Cave of Aglauros, a mythical Athenian heroine. Every year, the cadets of Athens—the ephebes—would go to that cave to take the Ephebic Oath, swearing to defend their city and to leave it not lesser but greater than how they received it.

Around Attica—Temples and Mysteries
Lecture 4

The countryside around Athens is known as Attica, and this tour takes us many miles into the Attic countryside—this is not a walking tour. Our jumping-off point for touring this beautiful landscape is the best-preserved classical monument in all of Athens: the Tower of the Winds. Built in the 1st century B.C., it stands in Athens's Roman agora, which is to the east of the classical-era agora we visited in our previous lecture.

- The Tower of the Winds is an octagonal structure, complete right up to its fantastic roof tiles. Donated by a wealthy patron, it served as a civic clock tower and as a weather vane. Weather vanes were very important to the seafaring Athenians.

- The panels are decorated with carvings of flying gods, each of which represents one of the eight winds: the north wind, Boreas, clad in warm clothing and blowing a conch shell; the west wind, Zephyros, a lightly clad young man pouring flowers onto the land below; the southwest wind, Lips, the god of good sailing who holds the stern of a ship; and so on.

- On the outside of the tower, little bronze pieces stick out from every corner, turning the whole structure into a massive sundial. Whatever angle you look at the tower from, the lines on the walls that mark the time are corrected so the shadow of those brass pieces shows the proper hour.

- Sundials, of course, are only useful in the daytime. Therefore, the Tower of the Winds also had a water clock. It consists of a tank filled slowly by a spring. As it fills, a bronze finger on a cork float rises and points to the hour as marked by horizontal lines on the tower walls.

- From the tower, head north to the shrine of the prophet Amphiaraus. His shrine is the Amphiareion, and the place is called Oropos. Although the shrine was technically in Boeotia under the rule of Thebes, the Athenians claimed the shrine as their own. Kings and city-states throughout ancient history fought to control such shrines.

- Amphiaraus was a prophet and one of the Seven Against Thebes, a group of legendary heroes who tried and failed to remove the usurper Creon from the Theban throne and restore Oedipus's sons to power.

- The gods decided to spare Amphiaraus a mortal death; instead, the land near the border of Boeotia and Attica swallowed him up, and the spot was marked with a sacred spring.

- The Amphiareion was an oracle and healing shrine right down to the Roman era and the arrival of Christianity. It is one of the loveliest spots in all of mainland Greece, with beautiful views and the ruins of a temple and theater.

- People came to the Amphiareion with an offering of a goat for the god. At the altar outside the temple, the goat was sacrificed, and the pilgrim was given its skin. That evening, he or she slept wrapped in that goat skin in a long stoa nearby, hoping that the god would visit in a dream.

- There is a water clock on a slope near the edge of the Amphiareion. It may have been used by the priests there to determine when their pilgrims' sleep was deepest and therefore the god most likely to visit. We do know that these priests woke the pilgrims in the middle of the night to ask about their dreams. The dreams were then written on a tablet and placed beside the dreamer, like a patient's chart in a modern hospital.

- Traveling down the east coast of Attica from Oropos, we reach the Gulf of Evia, which separates the island of Evia (or Euboea) from mainland Attica. Here we find several sights dedicated to goddesses. We do not know much about the cults that worshiped here because women in Greek society kept their rituals secret. The Greeks believed these secret rituals kept the state strong and healthy. If a man sought to discover women's rituals, he was put to death.

- Further along, we come to Rhamnous ("the place of the buckthorn") and the former sites of temples to Nemesis, the goddess of vengeance, and Themis, the goddess of justice. South of those sites, we find a shrine to Artemis, the virgin goddess of the hunt. Artemis's servants were little girls who were called bear cubs. They dressed as bears, danced, and made offerings. A few Doric colonnades still stand here.

- Next comes the mining district of Athens, called Lavrion or Laurion—"the place of silver." Ore was processed and coins were minted in the town of Thorikos. These coins, with Athena on one side and an owl on the other, were nicknamed owls. Athens was the only Greek mainland city that had large supplies of metal ores in its own territory. Be careful as you look down the old mine shafts that go hundreds of feet into the rock.

- At the southern tip of Attica, at Cape Sounio, we find the most spectacular of the Athenian shrines, that of the god Poseidon. Pausanias's guide to Greece begins with imagining the traveler on a ship seeing the colonnades of the shrine atop these 200-foot cliffs. The site offers spectacular views of the Saronic Gulf, particularly at sunset.

- Circling the cape and heading up the west coast of Attica, we come to a cluster of sites. The first of these is Piraeus, the port of Athens, four miles from the Acropolis. In the classical era, Piraeus and Athens were connected by a walled corridor that guaranteed the city could not be besieged.

- You can still see some of the walls along the corridor. At Piraeus, many of the structures are now submerged about 10 feet below the surface. A wonderful museum and two ancient theaters are also found here. The site is worth a full day's exploration in itself.

- The Byzantine monastery of Daphni also lies west of Athens. It contains some of the most fantastic frescos in the history of Byzantine art on its walls and dome.

Demeter, the Greek goddess of grain and fertility, is the central figure of the Eleusinian Mystery cult.

- Further north is Eleusis and a sanctuary to the classical Greek mother goddess, Demeter. It lies at the terminus of a sacred road that began at the Dipylon in Athens. Each fall, Athenians walked the nine or so miles to Eleusis to participate in initiation ceremonies there. Practitioners of the Eleusinian Mysteries had a much closer relationship to their goddess than the chilly, almost commercial interactions practiced at other Attic shrines.

- According to legend, a cleft in the rock at Eleusis is the place where Pluto kidnapped Persephone, Demeter's daughter. Demeter, in her grief, cursed the land, causing a drought. Ultimately, Demeter struck a compromise with Zeus, which led to the cycle of the seasons. Thus every autumn, when the rains returned to Greece, people all over the Greek and Roman worlds came to thank Demeter.

- The sanctuary was once the palace of a Mycenaean king who, according to the same legend, welcomed the mourning Demeter into his home. It was surrounded by high walls built in the 6th century B.C.

- The autumn festival was a multiday experience, including processions and purification rituals. The last ceremony took place in the Telesterion, a dark hall within the palace. No one knows the contents of the ceremony, but we do know that, without any drugs or other mind-altering chemicals, people were caught up in ecstasy and felt themselves reborn.

- This power over life and death prefigured the cult of Mithras during the Roman Empire and the ceremonies and beliefs of the early Christians. We do not know exactly what happened at Eleusis; we only know the experience was much more like our modern idea of a religious experience, a true emotional union with the deity, than the practices of other pagan cults.

Seeking the Good Life—Corinth to Epidauros
Lecture 5

The Peloponnese, in the southern half of Greece, is a great landmass shaped like a human hand with its fingers pointing south—great rocky capes reaching out into the Mediterranean Sea. It is connected to mainland Greece by a narrow isthmus; in fact, in ancient times the Spartans, Corinthians, and other Peloponnesian Greeks considered fortifying the isthmus to keep out Persians and other invaders from the north.

- The Corinth Canal cuts through the isthmus, connecting the Corinthian Gulf on the west with the Saronic Gulf in the east. It is one of the most amazing engineering feats to be seen in the entire Aegean world.

- The canal was originally envisioned approximately 2,000 years ago by the Roman emperor Nero, who wanted a way for his warships to pass unimpeded from the western to the eastern seas.

- Stop at the tourist station at the canal's edge and walk out on the bridge that carries the old road across the canal. Look down and marvel at the force of the vision, the skill of the engineers, and the determination of the diggers who got through this long passage of rock in the 1880s and 1890s.

- For another worthwhile view, take the road down to the eastern entrance of the canal, where you can see the unusual bridge at water level that spans the waterway. Rather than open like a drawbridge, this bridge sinks to allow ships to pass over it.

- On the southern (Peloponnesian) side of the canal is the Sanctuary to Poseidon at Isthmia. The Peloponnese is Poseidon's territory; it is not only a place where two seas meet, but it is somewhat prone to earthquakes, another of the god's domains.

- The sanctuary at Isthmia was the primary sanctuary to Poseidon in the ancient Greek world and was the site of special Panhellenic conferences, as when the city-states united against the Persians in 480 B.C.

- The Greeks held games in honor of the god here. In the remains of the stadium, you can see the stone threshold where runners would place their feet at the start of a race.

- Excavations at this stadium solved the mystery of how the ancient Greeks started races; little square holes beside each runner's place held posts, which held starting ropes.

- Before there was a canal, ships were hauled overland across the isthmus via a track called the *diolkos*. The Corinthians became wealthy by charging tolls for every ship that crossed.

- To get some idea of the glory of ancient Corinth, go straight south through the modern city to the gigantic acropolis, the Acrocorinth ("high Corinth"). The summit is home to a spring, now in an underground springhouse, called Peirene, which according to lore appeared when Pegasus struck this rock with his hoof. There was also once a shrine to Aphrodite here.

- The Acrocorinth has three rings of fortifications: The inner gates and walls are Byzantine; the middle ring, a little lower down, is Frankish from the era of the Crusades; and the outer circle with its monumental gate is from the time of the Ottoman Turks.

- In 146 B.C., the conquering Romans leveled Corinth. Except for a few sacred structures, the city was destroyed without trace.

- In the civic center of ancient Corinth, visit the remains of an extraordinary temple to Apollo, with its monumental Doric columns. Beyond that, you can see parts of the ancient Theater of Dionysus, which was spared by the Romans.

- The old city also shows evidence of Romanization. You will see some fantastic Roman-era mosaics from the homes of ancient Corinth's wealthy beautifully displayed in the site museum near the agora.

- During the Roman period, the Apostle Paul came to Corinth as a missionary. If you cross the agora to the Romans' place of judgment, you can stand in the same spot where Paul stood as Corinth's Jews denounced him to the Roman governor.

- Head southeast along the coast from Corinth toward the great pagan religious center of Epidauros. Along the way, you will pass the old Corinthian port of Kenchreai, now half sunk beneath the sea. You can still see some early Christian buildings, complete with mosaics, out in the surf.

- Further southeast, you will come upon the Sanctuary of Aesculapius at Epidauros, the principle shrine of the hero-god of healing. The propylaeum, the gateway into the site, links up with a sacred way to Palea Epidauros ("Old Epidauros"), a seaside town I urge you to visit.

- Epidauros has drawn pilgrims in search of healing for about 2,500 years. When you visit it today, you will see an extraordinary array of buildings.

- The modern emblem for medicine—a winged herald's staff with serpents coiled around it—comes from the cult of Aesculapius. Serpents were the servants of the god, the means of transferring his power to the afflicted person. We suspect that the tholos (circular building) inside the crypt area at Epidauros is where the sacred snakes lived. Look for the rings of stone masonry.

- Pilgrims slept in a large rectangular building adjoining the tholos area; its foundations are still visible. They hoped that the snakes would come to visit them either spiritually or physically while they slept, granting them dreams that would cure them or indicate they could be cured.

The Ancient Theater Festival at Epidauros

The magnificent, acoustically perfect ancient theater at Epidauros has hosted an annual summer theater festival for the past four decades as part of the Athens & Epidauros Festival. Performances at this site include the great works of ancient Greek playwrights and some Roman, Renaissance, and modern plays. For more information, visit http://www.greekfestival.gr/en/

- The main draw at Epidauros was its extraordinary theater, the best-preserved theater from the ancient world. Actors standing at the focal point of stage, even when speaking in a whisper, could be heard in the highest tiers of seats. A stone marks the focal point so you can try this for yourself.

- At the back of the orchestra area is a rectangular skene building, which housed cranes that would swing actors up to hang out over the stage, as if by divine power. We get our modern term *deus ex machina* ("god from the machine") from this practice. To the left and the right sides of the stage, you can see the chorus entrances, the parodoi.

Mycenae—Where Kings Planned the Trojan War
Lecture 6

Some 3,000 years ago, Mycenae was the very first capital of a united Greece—the only such capital from that time until the 19th century A.D. In Homer's *Iliad*, Mycenae was the citadel of the high king Agamemnon, who summoned the lesser Greek kings—Nestor, Odysseus, Diomedes, and Menestheus—along with 1,200 ships and thousands of men for an expedition across the Aegean Sea to Troy. Their mission was to rescue Queen Helen, the kidnapped wife of King Menelaus of Sparta, Agamemnon's brother.

- Not a single soul lives at Mycenae today. It is abandoned to the eagles, tourists, and archaeologists, and yet there is a unique spirit about it. Homer described the citadel as strong walled and rich in gold, and archaeology has proved him right on both counts.

- The stone ruins crouch atop a rounded mass of rock, expressing power, authority, and majesty. This was a strategic location in ancient Greece, on the road that ran from the plain of Argos to Corinth. Anybody who controlled this pass controlled the most important travel and trade route in ancient Greece. Tradition holds that the hero Perseus built the first castle here.

- Archaeologists first came to Mycenae when it was long deserted. In 1876, Heinrich Schliemann, just after his triumphant return from discovering the ruins of Troy, was given permission to dig at Mycenae to fill in the other side of the story—how the Greeks managed to unify and destroy of the mighty city of Troy.

- Mycenae is not closely described in the *Iliad*, so no one knew quite what to expect. The one clearly visible landmark was the Lion Gate. To reach it, we pass between the lowest circle of fortifications—dating to the 1200s B.C.—and an older, inner circle, until suddenly the gate looms over us.

- The Lion Gate is named for the pair of lions—probably lionesses—carved into in a triangular block of stone over its lintel. The triangle is part of the relieving arch that keeps the gate standing. Each of the opening's four stones—lintel, sides, and threshold—weighs about 20 tons.

- The lionesses frame a column that tapers from top to bottom. This is the emblem of the old gods of Minoan Crete and the Mycenaean religion—not centered around the Olympian gods but around a beneficent, omniscient mother goddess. She is a mistress of beasts who tames the lionesses and nature itself.

- There are post holes on either side of the threshold stone that held pivots on which wooden gates would have turned. Between about chest and waist height on either lintel stone are sockets for the mighty wooden bar that held the gates shut.

Mycenae's Lion Gate was the only visible landmark at the site when Heinrich Schliemann began digging there in the late 19th century.

© Photos.com/Getty Images/Thinkstock.

- To your left is a small hole in the wall that leads to a larger chamber. Opinion is divided among archaeologists as to whether this held an image of a guardian deity or was the guardhouse.

- Staircases run up the inside of the gate, giving access to the walls. As enemies approached, they were vulnerable to stones and arrows from soldiers stationed above.

- After the gate, you are confronted by one of the most spectacular elements in this citadel: the shaft grave circle, Schliemann's main dig at Mycenae. These square shafts were cut down to a depth of almost 25 feet. At the bottom, Schliemann encountered the skeletons of 19 individuals—men, women, and children— Mycenae's ruling dynasty.

- Gravestones were set over each shaft, showing images of war, hunting, chariot racing, and so forth, symbolizing each deceased's area of prowess. The royal family was also buried with treasures— about 30 pounds of gold in the form of crowns, masks, sword hilts, and more, not to mention the jewels.

- Five of the skeletons were adult men. Schliemann believed that one of these men was Agamemnon and that the gold mask he was buried with resembled his real face. But Schliemann was wrong. These shaft graves were from the Bronze Age, far earlier than the time of the Trojan War. They may, however, be from a dynasty founded by Perseus.

- We know something about the Bronze Age Mycenaeans from these skeletons. Their average age at death was a little under 40—not bad for the ancient world. They had good teeth and good overall health. From bone analysis, we know they ate a lot of meat, just as Homer describes in the *Iliad* and *Odyssey*.

- The shaft graves are surrounded by a strange double wall of stone, protecting the cemetery within the citadel but still protecting the living from spiritual "pollution" caused by close contact with the dead.

- As you climb up the walkway beside the shaft graves, look out over the lower parts of the citadel. You see some houses where we believe warriors, scribes, and other officials lived. Across the valley toward the car park, you see more buildings in the distance; these may have been lodgings for foreign visitors, such as traders or diplomats.

- Next we reach the palace gate. Entering the palace, we find a confusing jumble of rooms—the now roofless royal quarters, with views of the plain of Argos and even a glimpse of the sea.

- Next you will reach the Megaron, or great hall, which we might say is the room where the Trojan War was planned. It consists of an entry court, a circular hearth, and the throne of the king of Mycenae.

- The Megaron was also a feasting hall. But just as there is no free lunch in our world, there was no free dinner in the Bronze Age. By accepting a feast from the king, you made yourself a vassal or dependent. He could and did command his guests' loyalty. Mycenae, particularly this room, was the power hub of Bronze Age Greece.

- If you go to any Greek taverna today, you can order something called souvlaki (what the Turkish call shish kabob)—wooden skewers stacked with meat and vegetables cooked on a rack over a fire. A rack for cooking souvlaki was found at Mycenae; this dish is over 3,000 years old.

- Come over the top of the hill to enter the working part of the citadel where artists and craftsmen created status symbols—statues and figures, crowns and weapons—for the king to use or give as gifts to loyal subjects.

- At the far end is a lower courtyard and the postern gate, beyond which lie Corinth and northern Greece. A little doorway in the stone wall of the perimeter fortifications leads to a staircase of 99 stone steps down through the darkness to a cistern.

- This hidden water source, insurance against a siege, was constructed just before the collapse of Mycenae—and all of Mycenaean culture—at the hands of an unknown foe.

- Make sure to visit Mycenae's archaeological museum before leaving the site, but note that most of the gold objects in the museum are replicas. The real Mycenaean treasures are at the National Archaeological Museum at Athens.

- Replicas or not, the museum demonstrates the royal power and majesty of Mycenaean kings, the beauty and power of the mother goddess's votaries, and also how ordinary daily life was lived in the Bronze Age in the first united Greek state.

- One last point of interest lies outside the citadel. Schliemann was wrong about the shaft tombs inside the walls, but outside, dotting the landscape, are a number of tholi that did house the remains of Agamemnon's dynasty.

- One of these tholi is right near the museum. Entering that will help you understand these igloo-like stone structures; architecturally speaking, these are corbelled domes. The greatest of these domes, the Treasury of Atreus, lies on the right side of the road as you drive away from the main Mycenae site.

- A dromos, or runway, leads between high stone walls to the door of this tomb, which dates to about 1250 B.C.—too early for Agamemnon, but possibly belonging to Agamemnon's father, Atreus. During the Bronze Age, priests would have used this path to bring regular offerings to the dead king.

- The enormous lintel over the entrance is original, but the carved columns once flanking it are in the National Museum in Athens, and the triangular relieving arch has been lost. Inside, you will find a vast dome of stone, courses of corbelled masonry converging to a capstone far above your head, and a little inner burial chamber off to your right.

- After you have admired the interior, go out and climb to the top of the hill that conceals the dome to appreciate the architectural sleight of hand that allowed this manmade structure to look like part of the landscape.

Around Nafplio—Greek History at a Glance

Lecture 7

On your trip to Greece, if you are looking for one place to settle down for a while and soak up the experience of day-to-day life, go to the eastern Peloponnese to the Argolid, the area around the ancient city of Argos, and stay at the lovely port of Nafplio. From that base, you can explore a corner of Greece rich with relics of the Bronze Age and the classical, Roman, Byzantine, Venetian, and Turkish periods of Greek history, right up to earthshaking events that created the modern nation. All this is found side-by-side with wonderful swimming, snorkeling, boating, views, and hikes.

- Let's start our visit to the Argolid at a spectacular Mycenaean fortress called Tiryns. This fortress was linked to both the city of Argos and the citadel at Mycenae; the lords of Tiryns seem to have been Mycenaean vassals.

- Tiryns was built on a low hill by the sea where prehistoric peoples of the Neolithic (the Stone Age) had lived long before the warriors of the Bronze Age. These Stone Age people left behind pottery, figurines, and evidence of settled agriculture. In ancient times, the sea was much further away from Tiryns, but with the rise of the sea level, the Stone Age settlements were drowned.

- Homer called Tiryns "the place of the mighty walls." Its walls are built of big, rough stone blocks so immense that legend says the cyclopes built them. They have survived 3,000 years and counting.

- The approach to Tiryns is an uphill climb that leaves any potential invader exposed to attack from the walls. Never forget the warlike nature of Mycenaean society; most of their centers are fortified, but few as massively as Tiryns, perhaps because it is the closest to the sea.

- When you get through the gate, go left down the staircase and look into the gallery made of these same massive stones, with its pointed, vaulted roof and little windows that give it light and air. This was likely a storage room for weapons or a dwelling for the gate guards.

- You will notice that the rocks here seem to shine. This is the byproduct of hundreds of years of local shepherds sheltering their flocks in this room. The sheep rubbing up against these stones polished them to a glistening, lanolin-soaked smoothness.

- Like Mycenae, Tiryns was said to belong to Perseus the Gorgon slayer. It is also linked to the legends of Herakles (also known as Hercules), Perseus's great-grandson. Tiryns was one of the citadels of Herakles's brother, Eurystheus, for whom he performed his Twelve Labors.

- Next, climb back up the stairs and make your way to the area that was once the Megaron. You can see some of the column bases, as well as the circular hearth.

© iStockphoto/Thinkstock.

Just looking at Tiryns's Great Gate, we can understand why Homer called this citadel "the place of mighty walls."

- The top of Tiryns is bare; the upper walls are mostly gone. They may have been made of mud brick rather than stone.

- Go down the next flight of stairs to find the raised, elongated courtyard that was the domain of the palace servants, grooms, workers, cooks, craftspeople, and livestock. We know that the rulers of Tiryns also kept chariot horses here, thanks to the many frescoes that once decorated the walls but now reside in museums at Nafplio and Athens.

- The rulers of Tiryns used horses for warfare but also for leisure; the frescoes show them used for hunting wild boar and pleasure rides through the countryside. A network of roads connected Tiryns, Mycenae, and sites toward the Saronic Gulf through the hills to the north. Massive bridges were created in Cyclopean masonry along these roads, too.

- Around 1200 B.C., Greece's Bronze Age civilization somehow collapsed both on the mainland and on islands like Crete. During the following Iron Age, the countryside was depopulated. There were no major cities in Greece, the land was no longer worked regularly, literacy was lost, and the import of luxury goods tapered to almost nothing.

- We do not know what disaster caused this; archaeologists still argue about exactly what happened. What we do know is that after a few dark centuries, civilization began to bubble up again, centered on great timber halls, the seats of local strongmen.

- Through this dark age, the stories of the Mycenaean world endured in the songs of bards so that artists like Homer, who wrote during the 8th century B.C., would use them as the basis for their own works.

- In the museum in Nafplio, you can see a fantastic set of armor from the Bronze Age, discovered at a tomb in Dendra. It is made of circles of sheet bronze that hung from the wearer's shoulders. The helmet was like those described by Homer in the *Iliad*, decorated with the tusks of wild boars. Despite the link to Homer, this type of gear did not see use in the classical era.

- To see classical armor as it arose in the Argolid, visit the museum at Argos. The museum holds an 8th-century B.C. bronze breast plate complete with anatomical detail—defined pectoral muscles and a "six pack." The set includes a crested bronze helmet; most warriors would also have carried a great circular shield called an argive ("from Argos") shield, which would interlock with his fellow soldiers' shields as they advanced on the enemy as a phalanx.

- This sort of formation warfare may well have originated in Argos. Eventually, it made Greek troops, called hoplites, successful all over the Mediterranean and desired as mercenary troops in Babylon and Egypt.

- The spoils hoplite mercenaries brought back to Greece included not just wealth but ideas. These warriors were inspired by the songs of poets like Homer, the legendary tales of Bronze Age kings and warriors.

- Meanwhile, small communities centered on a strongman's great halls began to grow into what we call a polis—a Greek city-state—and Argos became one of the great ones.

- So why did Argos later fall into shadow? Because they developed distaste for the relentless, endless fighting of their neighbors, even remaining neutral in both the Persian Wars and the Peloponnesian War. Neutrals do not tend to make history.

- That said, Argos is well worth visiting. It was the site of many beautiful monuments, including a spectacular sanctuary to Hera to the east of the city called the Heraion. Here, several temples were built on terraces, commanding magnificent views out over the Argive Plain and the sea. Sadly, the most magnificent of these, from the classical era, burned down due to a priestess's carelessness. Most of the other buildings are gone now as well. Still, you can climb the terraces, look at the foundations, and see some magnificent views.

- The Argos museum also has some beautiful mosaics from the Roman period.

- South along the coast from Argos is a town called Eva where the greatest of all Roman-period villas was built in Greece during the reign of Emperor Hadrian by our friend Herodes Atticus, who built the odeon on the slopes of the Acropolis.

- The villa demonstrates just how thoroughly the Roman lifestyle was imposed on—or adopted by—the Greeks. While Greek culture–loving Romans were lavishing their attention on the monuments of ancient Greece, some Greeks were achieving tremendous wealth and aping the Romans.

- Argos was also important during the Byzantine period—that is, after Constantine moved the Roman capital to Constantinople. On the Acronafplio, the acropolis of Nafplio, you can see remains of Byzantine stonework fortifications.

- Nafplio was an important trading port for Byzantine merchants and remained a Byzantine base until the 1300s A.D., when the Venetians invaded. The Ottoman Turks and Venetians seized Nafplio from each other in turns for the next four centuries.

- The grid of streets that can be viewed from the Acronafplio today are the legacy of Venetian Renaissance planners. Walking around Nafplio, you will see many marks of the Venetian presence, including carvings of the winged lion of Saint Mark, the patron of Venice.

- Out in the harbor, which the Venetians helped create, is a little Venetian castle on an island called Bourtzi, which can be visited by boat. Back on the mainland you will find the Venetian-built Palamidi Fortress, finished in 1714 and captured by the Turks in 1715.

- By 1715, Nafplio and the rest of Greece was a province of the Ottoman Empire, and so it remained until 1821 and the Greek War of Independence. That war started at Nafplio, which became the first capital of the new nation of Greece.

Ancient Olympia—Gods, Games, and Temples
Lecture 8

O ne tiny site that had a tremendous impact on our modern world is the Sanctuary of Zeus and Hera at Olympia. Although named for Mount Olympus, the home of the gods in the classical era, the shrine's origins go back to the Bronze Age, when a series of athletic competitions were established as a form of worship—the ancestor of our Olympic Games.

- Present in this idea of the games in honor of a god are two conflicting elements of the Greek personality. One is a love and an admiration for *agon*, or contest, as the true measure of a person. The other is Panhellenism, an all-embracing Greekness.

- Every fourth summer, Greeks from the Black Sea all the way to the western Mediterranean came to this remote spot in the western Peloponnese to take part in five days of celebrations, rituals, and games. Months before, the athletes came to Olympia for a mandatory period of pregame training. The thousands or tens of thousands of spectators followed a few months later.

- Today, a modern town of Olympia has grown up outside the sacred sanctuary and the archaeological site, meaning you can easily get a hotel in walking distance. It is best to visit in the afternoon, when the day starts to get cool and the light golden.

- To get to the site from town, you will cross a bridge over the Kladeos, one of two rivers at whose convergence the sanctuary of Zeus and Hera sat. The archaeological museum will be to your left and the site straight ahead.

- The Olympic tradition began, according to the Greeks, in the year 776 B.C., the era of Homer and the rise of the Greek city-state. The games became such landmarks in the Greek world that they counted time with them, as in "such-and-such occurred in the third year of the 58th Olympiad."

- Ultimately, there were almost 300 Olympiads, the last occurring toward the end of the Roman period and the arrival of Christianity.

- Entering the site, immediately on the left is a Prytaneion, a building for the presiding officers to reside in. There was no village of Olympia in ancient times; the nearest city-states, Elis and Pisa, fought over the right to control the games, and one or the other would be in control at any given time.

- On the right is the practice gymnasium, a space so enormous it is hard for us to recognize it as a building. It held a running track that matched the length of the competition stadium on the other side of the site, about 630 feet long. There was also practice room for the field athletes, like javelin and discus throwers.

- Moving forward to our left we come to the Philippeion; the tholos is a latecomer to the site, from the late 4th century B.C. Its Ionic columns originally held a dome. Inside were the portraits of King Philip II of Macedon, his wife Queen Olympias, and their son Alexander, eventually known as Alexander the Great. This was a bit of Macedonian propaganda, an assertion of the house's Hellenic identity despite its northern roots.

- At the same time if you look to the right, you see the Palaestra, a small square open to the sun surrounded by colonnades and changing rooms, where wrestlers, boxers, kick boxers, and pankratiasts (which means the all-in fighters who fought to the death), and pentathlon competitors trained.

- Beyond the Palaestra is the workshop of the great Athenian sculptor Phidias, where the sanctuary's gigantic statue of Zeus was originally made in the 5th century B.C. This wooden sculpture covered with gold and ivory was considered one of the Seven Wonders of the Ancient World. Many of Phidias's tools were found during the excavation.

- The site of Olympia is well preserved for two reasons. First, it was covered by successive flooding of the Alfeios and Kladeos rivers, which covered the ruins in somewhat protective mud. Also, since there was no town at Olympia at that time, no one carried away the stone for other purposes.

- The temple that housed Phidias's enormous statue was turned into a Christian church during the very early Christian period. Its remains on a high stone podium. Most of the damage you see was done by an earthquake. In the northwest corner, a new column gives you a sense of the height and majesty of the original colonnades.

The Spirit of Sportsmanship?

An American bishop created the expression of the modern Olympic ideal that says it is not the winning but the taking part that counts. Nothing could be more alien to the ancient Greek idea of *agon*. The games at Olympia and elsewhere were all about winning. There were no second prizes. Winners were lavished with feasts and gifts and remembered in statues and stories; losers returned home in shame. This sort of arrogance in victory is mirrored in the poems of Homer. Read the way his heroes talk to each other, and you will find the origins of our modern tradition of trash talking at athletic events. That is much closer to the ancient Greek ideal.

- At the far eastern end of the temple, you will find a triangular column base that originally held the statue Winged Victory (Nike) of the Messenians commemorating a combined Messenian-Athenian victory over the Spartans in 425 B.C. So the spirit of Panhellenism was not always perfect.

- North of the temple, we enter an open space where the flame is kindled for the modern Olympic torch. The sun's rays are caught in a highly reflective bowl filled with tinder. Once the bowl gets hot enough, the contents burst into flame. There is no evidence of any such ritual for the ancient games.

- To the left of the torch site is the Temple of Hera. It is older than the Temple of Zeus; games for the girls and women in honor of Hera were held here long before the games for men.

- Each column of this Doric structure is different, because each was made at a different time by a different sculptor to replace the original, wooden columns as they rotted away. It is an interesting change from the clockwork precision of most classical Doric structures.

- Turn your back to the Temple of Hera and head east to enter the stadium proper. The 40,000 or so spectators would have climbed the earthworks to take their places; competitors entered through the vaulted corridor. Remarkably, this corridor is a true vault, including true arches, built by Greeks long before the supposed invention of such structures by the Romans.

- As you walk in, on the right you can see the area where the high priests and judges sat. You can also see the stone sill that was the starting line for the runners and fit your feet into the grooves they used.

- Come out again through the tunnel and notice some pedestals for statues lining your exit. Each held the statue of a cheater. The penalty for cheating at Olympia was to pay to have a statue of Zeus made and erected there so that you could be mocked and reviled for all time to come.

- Olympia boasts two wonderful museums. The Museum of the History of the Ancient Olympic Games has marvelous things like plaques listing the names of the winners. The second, the Archaeological Museum of Olympia, has remains of the tools from Phidias's workshop, magnificent sculptures, and the remains of objects buried as offerings to Zeus and Hera.

- The museum also contains a small sanctuary where you will find a beautiful statue of Hermes holding the baby Dionysus, created by the Athenian sculptor Praxiteles in the 4th century B.C. This same statue, which once stood in the Temple of Hera and was rediscovered in the 19th century, was described by Pausanias in his travel guide.

Quest for Wisdom at Apollo's Oracle—Delphi

Lecture 9

Delphi, the sanctuary of Apollo, is perched on the southern slope of Mount Parnassus in the very heart of Greece. It is the seat of the ancient oracle of Apollo, which was consulted over the course of thousands of years by ancient people from the Mediterranean world and beyond.

- The town of Delphi, with its spectacular views of the Corinthian Gulf and the mountains, as well as some of the most pleasant tavernas and workshops in all of Greece, is an attraction in and of itself.

- Your first stop at the shrine of Delphi should be the sacred spring, Kastalia, which is located outside the site. This bubbling, frothing spring was the place of purification both for the Pythia (the oracle priestess) and pilgrims.

- Across the road from the spring, you can look down on the Lower Sanctuary, which was used for sacrifices to Athena and purification rituals. Athletes who were competing in the Pythian Games in honor of Apollo also had their practice running track and bath house on that lower shelf of the mountain.

- Moving along the slope of the mountain to the west, you will come to the gates of the sanctuary. In ancient times, the seventh day after the new moon was holy to Apollo and was the day of consultation, the only day the Pythia entered the temple.

- The Pythia sat on a tripod in the heart of the temple. Having purified herself at the spring and fasted for three days, she would breathe in vapors coming up from the rock of Mount Parnassus, thus entering an altered state and becoming a medium through which the god would speak.

- The first thing a modern visitor encounters on entering the site was not there in the classical period; it is a Roman forum. Delphi was a tourist attraction for the Romans—one of the world's first, complete with professional tour guides. You can tell this is a later addition because it is made of brick, which the classical Greeks did not build with.

- Souvenirs were sold in this area: statuettes of Apollo; models of the Pythia's tripod; copies of the omphalos, the belly-button stone that marked the center of the world, which Delphi claimed to be.

- At dawn, the temple's priests lined up visitors in order of social precedence: generals, heads of state, ambassadors, and famous athletes were at the front of the line, ordinary folk behind them. They were led through a gate in an enclosing wall in a long procession.

- The pavement you walk along today was paid for by the Romans, probably by Emperor Hadrian. Notice the stones are grooved to make the ascent less slippery. This was not just for the visitors' benefit; it was so the sacrificial goats could keep their footing. A goat that shuddered, acted fearful, or stumbled was an unfavorable sacrifice, and the consultations would be cancelled for the day.

- There was plenty of entertainment for waiting visitors: a theater, athletic events, talks by philosophers, and the company of travelers from all over the world. Religion was a huge economic boon for this little mountain town.

- Continuing toward the temple, you will find the first switchback lined with war memorials and treasuries (rectangular buildings where pilgrims would leave offerings) of different Greek states on either side.

- Ascending some ramps and steps, we come to a beautiful shrine on our left, the Treasury of Athens. Archaeologists were able to reconstruct this treasury mostly intact, and on the outside of it, a hymn to the sun, Helios, had been engraved in ancient times. Luckily, the engraving includes musical notation, so musicians can reproduce the hymn, too.

- Also at the switchback, we see an omphalos stone, the emblem of the shrine. According to the Delphians, when Zeus released his two sacred eagles from the ends of the world and told them to meet in the middle, Delphi was the spot where they met. Zeus set the sacred stone there to mark the middle of his creation. This is not the real omphalos, however; the real one is inside the temple.

- A bit past the treasury, you will see a tumble of rocks and a fig tree. Wherever you see a fig tree, you can be pretty sure there's groundwater underneath. Here the groundwater is the original sacred spring and shrine of mother earth, Ge, from whose name we get the words "geography" and "geology."

- According to legend, when Apollo was a brand-new god, he came to this spot where Ge had been sending people prophetic dreams and decided to take over. Apollo killed Pytho, Ge's great she-dragon who guarded the site. Apollo and his priests then took over; Ge was demoted.

- You will also see nearby the big rock where a Sybil prophesized for a while. The Greeks believed that anyone could be filled with a prophetic spirit here if the god willed it.

- The last monument is on the left. The Stoa of the Athenians is a lovely set of steps crowned by a row of Ionic columns. This was a war monument that held Athenians victory trophies from naval battles.

- The back wall of the stoa is inscribed with the names of freed slaves, recording their emancipation. The ex-slaves deliberately placed these inscriptions in this sanctuary where it would be an act of sacrilege to deface or erase them.

The Spirit of the Earth

The ancient Greeks had claimed there was a crack in the mountainside at Delphi where vapors arose that put the Pythia into a trance. For 100 years, Western archaeologists and classicists said this was a myth. There was no gas. The Pythia's oracles were self-induced nonsense at best and a confidence game at worst.

Recently, however, geologist Jelle Z. de Boer found a fault beneath the Temple of Apollo at Delphi and, with my help, mapped out the length of the fault. We brought in chemists and toxicologists to analyze the traces of gasses coming from the fault. Dr. de Boer and I were able to show after several years of work that the rocks below the sanctuary are bituminous limestone laden with petrochemicals. When heated by the movement of the fault—the same fault that triggered the earthquake that knocked down the temple—the petrochemicals vaporized and rose to the surface through the crack over which the temple had been built.

Plutarch, the ancient Greek author who had been high priest at the temple, claimed that the gaseous emissions smelled sweet; indeed, one of the gasses we discovered at that fault is ethylene, which is also found in ripening fruit and does smell sweet. A person who inhaled these vaporized petrochemical gasses would certainly experience an altered state that the ancient Greeks interpreted as the touch of the god.

The Greeks were very sensitive to landscape. They read it as we would read a book. At Delphi, the fault, the spring, and the vapors told them that this site was holy. The temple was not built here by accident.

- Around 372 B.C., the original temple at Delphi was destroyed by an earthquake. The priests sent messengers all over the Greek world asking for contributions to rebuild the temple, promising all donors would have their names inscribed in the temple. The names have been found by archaeologists, along with donation amounts. In some cases, the amounts given were less than the cost of inscribing the name, yet the priests remained true to the promise.

- Make the final ascent to the site of the oracle herself. Note, it was a rare privilege to be allowed to enter a Greek temple. Most temples were entered only by the priests or priestesses who served the god. Ordinary people made their sacrifices outside the temple, on an altar like the one you see to your left. Delphi was a different sort of temple. The people entered the holy of holies itself to speak directly to the god and ask for guidance.

- There were two mottos on the outside of the temple. The first was *Gnothi seaton*, "know thyself," the message of Platonic philosophy, but it is also a warning. The god here at Delphi neither conceals nor reveals the truth. He gives a sign; you must know yourself to interpret it correctly. The second motto was *Meden Agan*, "nothing too much." There we have Aristotelian philosophy and another warning about how to react to the oracle's advice.

- Somewhere straight ahead as you enter would have been the site of an eternal flame tended by priestesses of Apollo, descendents of Ge's priestesses. The Pythia was chosen from their number. All around the temple, offerings were hung—chariots, shields, weaponry, works of art, golden bowls from foreign monarchs, gifts to the temple from grateful pilgrims of the past.

- When a pilgrim's name was called, he or she would pass the holy flame and descend a ramp or staircase to the crypt where the Pythia was seated. Somewhere ahead of us, at the upper level or down in the crypt, was a solid gold statue of Apollo, the cult image of the god. This was the cella, the heart of the temple.

- The cella would have been occupied by priests and, on most occasions, a *prophetes*, from which we get our word "prophet." The *prophetes* would take the Pythia's cryptic ramblings and write an improved version down on a tablet, which the questioners could take with them. The *prophetes* might translate the oracle into poetry, even, for a fee.

- To the south was a niche not much bigger than a phone booth where the Pythia sat on her tripod stool. She was in a trance but able to sit upright, holding a laurel branch and a dish of sacred water. When a question was asked, she made her cryptic response in a low, raspy voice.

- After you exit the temple, you will find a flight of steps at the back that will take you to a good viewing site.

© iStockphoto/Thinkstock.

Dionysus, god of theater, ruled Delphi in winter, and so there is also a great theater.

- Some visitors find the temple at Delphi a disappointment. There was not much left when the first French excavators came to restore the site in the 1890s. But as a compensation for the absence of architecture, Delphi seems to be returning to nature, to mother earth. The higher you ascend through the site, the more you will feel that.

- Beyond the temple is the beautiful Theater of Dionysus, Apollo's half brother who ruled Delphi in the wintertime. Above the theater are the areas that many tourists never explore, the sacred spring and a fabulous stadium with much of its seating still intact.

- The last Pythia gave her last oracle to the Emperor Julian the Apostate in the mid-4th century A.D.: "Go tell the king the fair-built hall has fallen." Apollo has no temple here, no sacred tree, no talking spring. The water of speech is silent. Yet for each of us who visits Delphi today, the magic of these surroundings allows the spirit of antiquity to speak again to each of us for a little while.

Byzantine Outposts—Monemvasia and Mistra

Lecture 10

In his poem "Sailing to Byzantium," William Butler Yates describes the search for a lost city, a realm of gold and young love—"no country for old men." That Byzantium vanished with the end of the Byzantine Empire in the 15th century A.D., but some outposts of Byzantium live on, carrying the city's spirit to our own time.

- An extraordinary mass of rock juts out from the eastern coast of the Peloponnese—Monemvasia, an outpost of that old Byzantine Empire that is still inhabited and where little has changed from Byzantine times.

- Arriving by boat, visitors make landfall at a stone wharf and climb a flight of steps to the Portillo, the old arched water gate in the city wall.

- Inside, the city is a maze of tiny streets and lanes so narrow that two people cannot walk in them side by side. The streets give up the fight with the slope and become steps, which in turn lead to a tiny square surrounded by buildings of the Byzantine Empire.

- Monemvasia was a great trading center founded in A.D. 581 by Greeks fleeing unsettled conditions on the mainland Peloponnese. Its ancient name, Minoa, comes from King Minos of Crete. It was probably a trading colony of a far away power even in ancient times. The name "Monemvasia" means "one way in," referring to the little spit of land that connects the rock to the mainland.

- The Byzantine walls enclose a slice of history, a place where the patterns of life and the architecture of the long-lost Byzantine world are still all around us in the form of private houses, churches, and fortifications.

- From the lower town, walk up a precipitous flight of steps between some ordinary houses that develops into a switchback trail up a precipice, lined with parapets that make sure you do not plunge to your deaths in the town below. You will pass under archways and see old wooden doors that appear to be as old as the Byzantine Empire.

- At last you will emerge onto a sun-baked, treeless summit surrounded by scrub, thorns, and tiny flowers. Above are the ruined walls of the Byzantine citadel and a Byzantine church. This Greek Orthodox church is called Hagia Sophia, a less-famous little sister to the great mosque in Istanbul of that name, and was built in the 12th century A.D.

- On approach, the church seems to be hanging in space, with sheer drops to the sea below. The building shows all the hallmarks of Byzantine architecture. Compared to the light, open architecture of the Greeks and Romans, this is an enclosed brick building, rising to a dome and a tiled roof. Tiny arched windows let in a bare minimum of light. It seems like a deliberate rejection of the classical, pagan world.

- Inside, the church is dim and shadowy. Traces of ancient frescoes can be seen on the walls; those once adorning the dome are gone, but viewing the dome itself is a beautiful, heart-soaring experience nonetheless. The Byzantine architects were seeking to produce a sense of transport and elevation in those who worshiped here.

- After exploring the church and the summit, climb down the switchback trail once again into the town. Monemvasia is the home of malvasia, a sweet white wine also known as malmsey. The Portuguese developed a taste for this wine and carried the grapes and the style to the island of Madeira.

- Settle in at a sidewalk café with a bottle of malvasia and take in the architecture for a while. From this vantage point, you can see that more than one civilization has left its mark here. Monemvasia was a strategic location that changed hands many times over the centuries.

- In the town square, beside the Byzantine church, you will find a great campanile of a Venetian bell tower. Nearby is an Ottoman mosque.

- One of the adventurers who captured Monemvasia was a Frankish lord named Guillaume of Villehardouin. He came in the middle of the 13th century. His next stop in the southern Peloponnese was Mistra, and it is our next stop as well.

- Mistra (sometimes spelled Mystras) lies along the slopes of the central mountain ridge, at the foot of Mount Taygetos, just four miles from the ancient city-state of Sparta. William and his knights built a castle on a crag here, one of the most extraordinary castles in the Aegean, a medieval castle that looks like it was transported directly from the south of France.

- Some of the castle's stonework looks fine enough to be in a Gothic cathedral. No Byzantine bricks here; the castle is composed of finely cut stones hauled up an immense distance from the valley below.

- The curtain walls are still intact, marked by turrets, crenulated battlements, and arrow slits. But this is just a shell; you can try to imagine the beautiful life that went on in this castle.

- The Byzantines captured Monemvasia and Mistra from Guillaume just 10 years after he had conquered them. The castle at Mistra was so well-built and well-situated that the Byzantines decided to keep it and created the town of Mistra on the slope below.

- Far below the Frankish castle are the remains of the Byzantine palace. The arcades of windows and lovely stonework are unlike Byzantine church architecture and give us an idea of the kind of palace architecture that has been lost elsewhere in the vanished empire.

- The L-shaped structure seems extraordinarily preserved on approach; unfortunately, like the castle, it is just a shell.

- Late in its history, there were still 40,000 people living at Mistra. They farmed the plain below; their most important industry was silk. Thus the plains below Mistra were covered in mulberry trees throughout the Middle Ages. The whole of the Peloponnese was ultimately called Morea, "mulberry leaf," not only for its shape but for its abundance of mulberry trees.

- The surviving churches and monastic foundations around Mistra demonstrate the glories of Byzantine ecclesiastical architecture. The nunnery of Pantanassa contains some of the most remarkable frescoes to survive from the Byzantine era. They demonstrate a change in style from flat, iconic Byzantine-type figures to a more rounded, three-dimensional Renaissance style, plus extraordinary color choices that make the figures seem to spring free of the background.

Tips for Touring Mistra

I urge you to start at the castle because from that lofty height, you can not only look down at a beautiful view of Byzantine Mistra spread out on the slope below; you will have an eagle's eye view of the whole vale of Laconia, the territory of the Spartans, and the Evrotas River winding through its green plains down to the distant Aegean Sea.

- Near Pantanassa is a monastery called the Brontochion, famous for one of its residents, George Gemistos Plethon. Plethon's mission was to revive interest in the Greek classics. He wrote a long book about Plato and Aristotle in which he showed how Aristotle was wrong about everything and Plato was right. The whole world got to know these two lost philosophers from his book, which had a tremendous impact on the Italian Renaissance.

- At the bottom of the hill, we come to the grand St. Demetrios Church. Inside, a white marble plaque on the floor, bearing the double-headed eagle emblem of the Byzantine Empire, marks the spot where according to tradition Constantine XI, the last emperor of Byzantium, was consecrated. Constantine lived at Mistra, as did many princes of the imperial house. The city was like a second Byzantium in the remote reaches of the empire.

- At the bottom of the hill, you will find yourself in a little town. Note that even the manhole covers have the double-headed eagle on them, as if the modern population is eager to proclaim their allegiance to that long-vanished empire.

- Today, Mistra is practically a ghost town, but that is not true of some other surviving outposts of Byzantium, particularly the monasteries. Meteora, an extraordinary geological formation in the Pindos Mountains, boasts an extraordinary set of Byzantine monasteries at its top. These sandstone towers near the town of Kalambaka were the refuge of monastic groups in the 13th century.

- Presently, Byzantine studies are on the rise in universities all over the world. Is this in part because this generation is beginning to feel more sympathy with the uncertain, beleaguered world of the Byzantines than with the stable, ordered classical world of Greece and Rome?

- I would like to share with you a personal encounter that I had with the Byzantine Empire at Mount Athos in the far north of the Aegean Sea.

  o The Mount Athos promontory extends like a finger down into the Aegean with the soaring mass of the mountain at its tip. On the slopes are many ancient monasteries reaching back to Byzantine times, where the rituals and devotions of Byzantium are still carried on.

  o On one occasion, I was hanging off my research vessel by a big crane, sitting in a submersible. I looked out and saw a Byzantine monk standing in a little boat, and I was concerned that we misunderstood our permit and had come too close to the sacred shore. But he was simply there to bless the boat, to offer an ancient prayer to protect us down in the deep.

  o That night, I sat on the deck of the ship and looked up at Mount Athos as the lights came on in all the monasteries. There I was, surrounded by all the technology of the modern world, leading a life that moves at a mile a minute, looking up to the men whose lifestyle went back hundreds of years. I asked myself, which way of life is truly the more enduring?

Cruising the Islands—Mykonos and Delos
Lecture 11

No visit to Greece and the Aegean is complete without a cruise around the islands. Each island is a world of its own. We begin with the full range of wonders to be found in the individual islands and archipelagos and then pick out a few of the best to discuss in more detail.

- A word of advice: Do not plan to cruise the Aegean in the winter. The Greeks did not go out on the rough and stormy sea in the winter months, nor should you. Nonetheless, in spring, summer, and fall, ferrying around the Aegean islands is a huge delight.

- In the far northwest, islands like Corfu offer a mixture of Greek and Italian culture, since the Italians long held Corfu as their own possession. South from Corfu, we find Kythera, home of the goddess of love and beauty—Aphrodite. At the southern edge of the Aegean islands is Crete, worth a major visit of its own, which we will pay it in a later lecture.

- Toward the coast of Turkey, we come to three big islands: Samos and Chios—both famous for their wines—and Lesvos, or Lesbos, home of the poet Sappho and one of the most amazing petrified forests on earth.

- Near the Greek mainland, north of Attica, is Evia, or Euboea, which exemplifies what is so remarkable about these islands: They are the peaks of a drowned mountain range.

- In addition to the big individual islands are archipelagos. One well-visited archipelago is found at the mouths of the Gulf of Corinth and the Gulf of Patras. This range includes Ithaca, Odysseus's home island; Kefalonia, offering beautiful beaches and a wonderful ancient citadel; Zakynthos, famous for its mineral springs; and Lefkas. You do not have to even get off the ferryboat to enjoy these islands.

- The Sporades are three islands—Skiathos, Skopelos, and Skyros—north of Euboea, guarding the approaches to northern Greece. They are wildly popular today with holiday seekers from Europe and America.

- In the southeastern Aegean is the Dodecanese Archipelago. The prefix *dodeca-* is Greek for 12, so this is an archipelago of 12 islands. It was home to one of the Seven Wonders of the Ancient World, the Colossus of Rhodes. The northern Dodecanese include Patmos, where Saint John wrote the book of Revelation, and Kos, where Hippocrates invented scientific medicine.

- In the heart of the Aegean Sea are the Cyclades, a group of islands that form a wheel whose hub is the island of Delos.

  ○ According to myth, Zeus chained Delos in place, making it the least earthquake-prone spot in the Aegean. We will revisit Delos shortly.

  ○ Part of the Cyclades, near Attica is the island of Sifnos, which was famous in the ancient world for its gold mines and was routinely raided by pirates. Today, the entrances to these mines are lost; they may now be below sea level. It is a beautiful, quiet spot.

  ○ South of Delos are a pair of islands: Naxos and Paros. Paros was famous in the ancient world its pure white marble, Naxos for its wine and almonds.

- One of the biggest free-standing doorways in the world stands on a rocky peninsula beside the port of Naxos. It is all that remains of an ancient Temple of Apollo, who was father god to the Ionian Greeks of the Cyclades.

- Elsewhere on Naxos, archaeologists are reconstructing a Temple of Demeter using some of the original, translucently thin slabs of Naxian and Parian marble.

- Further south again we come to the islands of Milos and Santorini. Milos is the home of the famous Venus de Milo sculpture. Santorini is a dramatic volcanic island reminiscent of the Grand Canyon. We visit them in detail in the next lecture.

- Before visiting the Cyclades, I recommend visiting to the Museum of Cycladic Art in Athens. There you can see the unique form of sculpture developed in these islands during the Neolithic and the Bronze Ages, where individual features and details are minimal and bold forms are emphasized. These statues inspired artists like Constantin Brancusi and Pablo Picasso.

- Mykonos is perhaps the most popular tourist island in the world, a stark contrast to its near neighbor Delos, which is silent, uninhabited, and dedicated to the gods and the past. Mykonos was a small fishing island until the 1960s, when Jacqueline Kennedy Onassis made it one of her favorite vacation spots—and by extension, a favorite of the world's elite.

- Mykonos's beaches are legendarily beautiful, but do not miss the archaeological, maritime, and agriculture museums, nor the beautiful countryside and the local churches, with their whitewashed walls and gleaming turquoise domes.

- Delos was not only the heart of the Cyclades; the Greeks believed this was the place where Apollo was born. The only way to reach Delos is by ferry from Mykonos. When you disembark from the ferry, go left (north) toward the shattered remnants of the ancient Sanctuary of Apollo.

- Somewhere in this tangle of marble ruins is the spot where the Delian League met in the mid-5th century B.C. This league, led by Athens, was a confederacy of Greek city-states that united in defense against the Persian Empire.

- A few landmarks stand out at this site. There is a beautiful avenue lined with replicas of statues of lions given to Delos by Naxos. They are so weathered by centuries out in the open that they now resemble stylized Cycladic sculptures. Also look for the purification pool and the base of what was once an enormous phallus, where the Greeks worshiped Apollo as the father of all.

- The treasury of Delos was filled with contributions from other Greek states but was ultimately moved to Athens, so the Athenians had enough money to build the Parthenon and the other great buildings of the Periclean architectural program.

- Near the ferry landing, you can visit the Archaeological Museum of Delos. It holds many fantastic sculptures and vases, but it also displays artifacts of everyday life.

- Delos got a second lease on life in the Hellenistic period when it became the main marketplace of Greece. Delos's location at the hub of the Cyclades made it a natural meeting place for merchants—one of several in the Aegean—but the destruction of Corinth by Rome in 146 B.C. left Delos without rivals. For the next half century, the people of Delos welcomed traders and merchants from almost 100 different communities around the Mediterranean.

- In the Hellenistic and Roman periods, the mosaic became a true art form, and you will see amazing mosaics in the remains of merchants' homes here. In particular, seek out the House of the Dolphins and the House of the Trident.

- Delos is an island almost without springs, which is why it never developed farms and villages. Houses on Delos got their water by trapping rainwater in fall, winter, and spring in underground cisterns and then drawing on that water throughout the dry summer months. The city also had an immense public reservoir; you still visit the immense vaults.

- Mount Kynthos is the central feature of the island. Halfway up the slope, you can visit what is probably the oldest place of worship on the island: Two immense lintel stones forming a massive stone gable, a basin for offerings or purification, and a sacred cave. This may have been an oracle site.

- From here you can see the entire island, from the Sanctuary of Apollo to the ruins of the Roman and Hellenistic community. Toward the horizon, you can see the islands of the inner Cyclades.

Aegean Ring of Fire—Milos and Santorini
Lecture 12

Two remarkable volcanic islands lie at the southern edge of the Cycladic archipelago—Milos and Santorini. While only 90 or 100 sea miles from Athens, they are worlds of their own. Milos is infrequently visited; Santorini is one of the most popular tourist destinations in the Mediterranean. But we are going to give them equal billing.

- Milos (from the Greek *melos*, "apple," after its shape) bears witness to the geologic drama of the collision between the African and European plates, which began some 25 million years ago. Milos is significantly more eroded than Santorini.

- The bay where you arrive on Milos is actually a crater, the caldera of this now sleeping volcano. It is an excellent harbor, and were it not for the lack of fresh water here, Milos might have become one of the great centers of Aegean civilization.

- Milos is a geologist's dream. Minimal vegetation leaves the many layers of rock exposed, showing veins of white pumice and black obsidian—volcanic glass—prized before the Bronze Age for its ability to take a sharp edge and in later eras for its beauty.

- Milos's distinctively chemically marked obsidian is found in ancient sites all over the Peloponnese, proving that Greeks from the mainland were sailing and trading in the Aegean more than 10,000 years ago. Volcanic minerals are still being extracted and mined here.

- The ferry landing is near the north end of the island, where all of the archaeological sites are. It is a good idea to get some transport unless you are fit and up for some exercise; walking on Milos is more like hiking.

- The main town of Milos, a place called Plaka, is high on a hill. You should visit its archaeological museum, where you will see the statue that represents Milos to the world—the Venus de Milo. (Actually, this is a plaster reproduction; the original is in the Louvre.)

- The statue was discovered on a nearby farm in 1820. From other pieces found at the site, we know her missing right hand once held a bit of her robes and her missing left hand held an apple—a reference to the incident that started the Trojan War.

- Go west from Plaka to the sea, where you will find an ancient classical theater. Although the theater is in ruins, it is a beautiful site, particularly in spring, when it is covered in wildflowers.

- The seating faces the water, giving an excellent view of the bay and the southern half of the island at any time of year. Originally, the skene would have blocked the ancient spectators' view of the sea and landscape.

- Near the theater, you can find the plaque that marks the spot where the Venus de Milo allegedly was discovered—"allegedly" because there are a number of conflicting stories about when she was found, what condition she was in, and how she passed from the Greek farmer into the hands of the French.

- The theater is also within walking distance of an important site in early Christian history—a set of catacombs, burial and possibly meeting places for Christians of the 1st century A.D. when Christianity was suspect, if not outright illegal, in the Roman Empire.

- The catacombs at Milos have not been precisely dated and were swept clean by looters before the archaeologists got there, but the inscriptions date to the 1st century, and the site may predate the catacombs of Rome. These catacombs contain 290 niches that may once have held as many as 2,000 bodies.

- Among the catacomb inscriptions is the word *ichthus*, meaning "fish," a code word early Christians used to identify each other. It was an acronym that stood for *Iesos Christos Theos Uios Soter*—"Jesus Christ, God's Son and Savior."

- One of the best times of year to visit Milos is Easter. (Note, here the Eastern Orthodox calendar is used to determine the date.) Local traditional religious festivals are celebrated throughout the year in Greece and Turkey, but Easter is the biggest. These festivals are a great opportunity to see traditional Greek dancing.

- East of Milos, Santorini looms up out of the sea. You can reach Santorini from Athens and many other points by airplane, but a ferry from Piraeus (near Athens) or Iraklio (on Crete) will reward you with a scene unlike any other on this earth: entering the crater of an enormous volcano, the cliffs gleaming in the sun, new vistas opening dramatically before you at every moment.

Milos, once a turbulent volcano, is now a quiet, peaceful refuge.

- The downside of the ferry is its landing along the southern shores of the crater, far from the sites you will want to see. You should arrange your Santorini transportation before you get on the boat; bring your car or motorbike with you, or have your hotel or a rental agency bring a car to the landing for you. You can rent donkeys as well, but I do not recommend them.

- In the middle of the caldera are a couple of tiny volcanic cones. While the bulk of Santorini is hundreds of thousands, perhaps millions of years old, in 197 B.C., a new volcano formed in the middle of the bay, creating the island we now call Palea Kameni ("Old Kameni").

- Next to Palea Kameni is Nea Kameni ("New Kameni"), a volcano that has been continuously active since A.D. 1707. Take a ferry out there and enjoy a walk on some of the newest land on earth, as well as a dip in the volcanic hot springs or mud baths.

- Another volcanic explosion in the 1620s B.C. destroyed Akrotiri, our modern name for a Bronze Age Minoan (Cretan) village on the southeastern slope of Santorini. The site was discovered by pozzolana miners. Pozzolana is a volcanic sand used to make cement.

- Akrotiri is the chief historical site on Santorini, but check to make sure it is open before you visit.

- Akrotiri's frescoes now reside in museums, but they demonstrate the residents' love for their landscape. They painted the volcanic rocks, wildflowers, and wildlife. They also recorded the everyday life of the island, from the lowly fishermen at work to sports and leisure among the upper classes. They show fleets of ships decked out for religious festivals and the fashions of ancient Akrotiri, including the unique hairstyles sported by their young men.

- The numerous frescoes indicate that the part of Akrotiri excavated was an elite neighborhood—the Beverly Hills of Akrotiri—but little else has been recovered from the site. The volcano's devastation was massive—another Pompeii.

- Like Pompeii, the residents of Akrotiri were warned of the coming destruction by an earthquake a few years earlier. Unlike at Pompeii, no human bodies were found at the site; at the time of the eruption, the town seems to have been abandoned by all but some construction workers, who we think were able to escape in time.

- In a few cases, it has been possible to reconstruct the furniture from Akrotiri using the same plaster casting techniques developed by the archaeologists at Pompeii. Most of the frescoes and other objects from the site are kept in a museum at Fira, Santorini's principal tourist town.

- Fira, in the center of the caldera, is also the main port for cruise ships, a real party town, and home to many beautiful churches and wonderful cafés. On the northern tip of the island is the town of Ia (sometimes spelled Oia), a much quieter place. It is a great place to sit on the edge of the crater and watch the sun set while sipping a glass of the local wine, tinged with the flavors of the volcanic soil.

Exploring Crete—Realm of Ancient Minoans
Lecture 13

C rete is the greatest of all the Aegean islands and the place where Europe begins, not just geographically but historically. Its great Minoan civilization, named for the legendary King Minos of Knossos, gave the West its distinctive cultural qualities. In fact, in my opinion, it is only because of Crete that Europe can be considered a continent at all, in that the difference between Europe and Asia is more a cultural divide than a geographical one.

- Most visitors approach Crete from the north by ferry or plane to the ancient port of Iraklio, also called Heraklion, "the place of Herakles." The remains of the Bronze Age port are dwarfed by the more modern harbor, commercial town, and touristic center.

- You must visit the archaeological museum of Iraklio if you are anywhere in the neighborhood with even one hour to spend. This collection of artifacts drawn from all over Crete will dazzle you with gold, rock crystal, bronze, and pottery from the Neolithic through the late Bronze Age.

- Iraklio still shows the impress of its Venetian conquerors in its very deliberate layout created during the Renaissance. Iraklio was one of their main fortresses; the Venetian castle, with its crenellated bastions and winged lion of Saint Mark over the gate, is visible from the ferry port.

- As you ascend the hill into the city proper, you will discover again that the Venetians have left their mark in the very center of the town at the Place of the Lions. Its centerpiece is a fountain where four stone lions spout water into a beautiful Renaissance basin.

- Nearby is the town hall, which is also the old Venetian palace, and the Church of St. Titus, the patron saint of Crete, who was the island's first bishop, sent by Saint Paul himself.

- This wonderful Venetian cityscape is still surrounded by the Venetian walls, punctuated by massive bastions projecting like spear points out into the countryside. The biggest, most formidable, and incidentally southernmost of these bastions is called the Martinengo.

- Martinengo is also the last resting place of one of Crete's most important sons, Nikos Kazantzakis, author of *Zorba, the Greek* and *The Last Temptation of Christ*. A notorious freethinker, he is buried here because he was excommunicated and denied burial rights in consecrated ground.

- With Iraklio as a base of operations, there are three excellent excursions you can take around Crete—one east, one south, and one west.

- Traveling east, past the airport, along Crete's north shore, we stop at the first of our Minoan palaces, Malia. It is unusual among the Minoan palaces for being built on flat land and very near the sea. Built around 1900 B.C., it was destroyed in an island-wide earthquake around 1700 B.C. These are, not coincidentally, the basic dates for the first phase of the Minoan palace-building period.

- After the earthquake, the Minoans rebuilt bigger and better than before and enjoyed some two-and-a-half centuries of glorious, civilized life. This carries us down to about 1450 B.C., when there appears to have been another island-wide disaster.

- In the third Minoan palatial period, the central palace at Knossos seems to have become the high seat of government, and all the other palaces, like Malia, lost their independence as a new set of actors emerged on the scene.

- The Minoans themselves were not Greek. They were not even Indo-European; that is, we know from their script—which we call Linear A, and which has never been deciphered—that their language was not an Indo-European one.

- They arrived about 10,000 years ago from Anatolia, bringing crops and livestock. Their great contribution to world cuisine was the domestication of the wild olive trees they found growing all over Crete.

- In 1450 B.C., they were conquered by people from the European mainland, people with whom they had shared all the gifts of their civilization—the Mycenaean Greeks, who invaded, spread all over Crete, and ruled from Knossos until the Greek dark ages, starting around 1200 B.C., when the island was depopulated and the palaces abandoned.

- At Malia, you should notice a couple of things. In addition to the grand ceremonial courtyards, warrens of rooms, and storage chambers typical of all the palaces, notice the double-ax symbol, the labrys. This was the sacred emblem of Minoan Crete, which gave its name to the Labyrinth.

- Beyond Malia, we come to Agios Nikolaos, a beautiful little town with a unique central water feature—a freshwater pool, unfathomably deep, with waterfalls pouring into it and picturesque cliffs around it. It is surrounded by a set of restaurants and cafés where you can take a pleasant meal break.

- Agios Nikolaos has a nice museum and also offers access to the ancient Minoan town of Gournia and the former leper colony of Spinalonga on an island off the coast.

- On the far eastern end of the island is Zakros, a Minoan palace that was never looted but simply abandoned. Incidentally, it is the best place in the Aegean to watch the sun come up over Asia, far away over the eastern Mediterranean.

- Our second excursion takes us south around the island. It can be done in a single day if you start early. Head first for the old city of Gortyn, or Gortys, in the middle of the island, the Roman capital of Crete.

- Gortyn is a large and confusing site, so ask one of the site staff for directions to its two best features: the Roman odeon and the Basilica of St. Titus.

  o Built into the wall of the odeon is one of the most important elements defining Crete as the place where Europe began: the oldest written law code in Europe. Written in ancient Greek script and carved around 500 B.C., it contains hundreds of different laws, mainly about marriage, contracts, and property.

  o The basilica is the site where Crete's first Christians would have worshiped. Most of the chancel area is still standing, and it is easy to make out the three aisles that are the classic mark of Roman basilica architecture.

- Our next destination, south of Gortyn, is the great palace of Phaistos, second only to Knossos in grandeur. It offers views of the horned summit of Mount Ida along the axis of its central courtyard, but like all Minoan palaces, inside it is a confusing warren of rooms. It is easy to see why the ancients associated the people of Crete with mazes and labyrinths.

- Enter the site by descending the steps and turning left, skirting the great mound. You will come to a collection of storage rooms and work rooms where an extremely important artifact was discovered in the early 20th century: the Phaistos Disk.

- At first, because the layers of earth at the site were jumbled, it was not clear whether the disc was Hellenistic (from the first few centuries B.C.) or Minoan (pre-1450 B.C.), but the images on the disk proved it to be the latter.

- The disk is an example of the first use of movable type in Europe. Centuries before Gutenberg, someone stamped this clay disk with a two spirals of pictograms—30 on one side, 31 or the other. They suggest a writing system of which no other trace has survived, although they resemble images found on Cyprus; some think the disk is a 20th-century fake.

- There are regular scholarly meetings about it, and a whole literature has sprung up trying to explain and decipher the symbols. Sir Arthur Evans believed it was a hymn to the sun goddess. Nonetheless, they remain a mystery to this day.

- Wandering toward the heart of the ruins may leave you feeling disoriented—this may even have been the architects' intent. But at the center of it all, suddenly everything will open in front of you in the central court.

- This area may have been used for ceremonies and gatherings, including the bull dancing seen in Cretan frescoes, where athletic men and women vaulted over the animals' horns. These death-defying dances may have been a combination between religious ritual and sporting entertainment.

- Around the courtyard, you can see the below-ground storage areas, where the giant and beautifully decorated pithoi are displayed. Many were fired with decorative cords worked into the clay, giving a hint as to the kind of rope used to carry them in Minoan times.

- The stone walls still hold a few traces of red and white paint, which give us a sense of how glorious and colorful such palaces were in their heyday.

- End your tour in the palace's other courtyard, where a processional way is marked out in stone slabs and broad steps leading off into the distance.

- You might want to end your day down by the beach, or you can go a few miles west to Agia Triada, a little cluster of Minoan villas and a ceremonial center.

- Matala Beach has some archaeological interest. In ancient times, masons cut chamber tombs in the northern cliff for Romans to be buried in. Matala Bay was also the port for Phaistos, where in Minoan times goods were brought from and sent to lands as far away as Egypt.

- If you have time for only one excursion on Crete, you may want to take our third tour and go west from Iraklio along the coast.

- You first come to Rethymno, where you will find Venetian palaces in a quarter near the harbor, full of lovely little lanes and squares with fountains playing in the middle.

- Next along the coast is Chania, an ancient Greek city that became the Venetian capital of Crete. Once fought over by Greeks, Romans, Venetians, Turks, and Arabs, the scars of its many wars have now mellowed into the grand facades of old Venetian houses reflected in the blue water and the remains of arsenals.

- One of the extraordinary wonders of Europe lies just south of Chania: Samaria Gorge, the longest ravine in Europe. Here you see Europe as it was 10,000 years ago, after the end of the last ice age.

- Fierce rivers have cut narrow gorges downward to the sea; you are walking along one of them, surrounded by wildflowers if it is spring or early summer. Some of these flowers grow nowhere else in the world. If you are lucky, you will catch a glimpse of a kri kri, the wild goat of Crete, native to the island and also found nowhere else on earth.

- The cliffs rise to 1,500 feet on either side of the gorge, which in some places narrows to only 10 feet and at others widens to 150.

- Among the glories of the Samaria Gorge are the stands of wild cypress growing out of the rock, reminding us that some of the cypress found in Egyptian sarcophagi came from Crete, some of it perhaps from this very gorge.

- After a walk that may take from five to seven hours, you will find yourself at a beautiful beach where the gorge emerges into the Mediterranean. Of course, there will be a spot for you to grab a drink or a meal there; then you can take a bus back to Chania.

- Before you go, take a moment to look around you and reflect that you are seeing Europe as it was at the beginning, before successive civilizations left their marks on the landscape. Also, reflect that the very first civilization to do so was born right here on the island of Crete.

Lure of the Labyrinth—Palace at Knossos
Lecture 14

The Palace of Knossos is one of the most daunting yet rewarding of all archaeological sites. Situated on the north-central coast of Crete, it stands among sites like Ur in Iraq and Copan in Honduras where an entire civilization lost and forgotten has been brought back into the historical record by an archaeological discovery.

- Knossos was discovered by Sir Arthur Evans, a wealthy Englishman. Inspired by Heinrich Schliemann's discovery of Troy, he followed the legends and, in 1900, bought the land where King Minos's palace was supposed to have stood.

- It is easy to get to Knossos from Iraklio—a quick three miles inland by bicycle, bus, or car. I strongly recommend that you buy a map and even a guidebook at the site itself, which will explain the site's many points of interest.

- Knossos is a large site, so comfortable walking shoes are a must. It is also a very open site. Remember your hat, sunscreen, and water!

- If you really want to get a lot out of your visit, consider hiring a freelance guide. These professionals are thoroughly trained and licensed by the Greek government.

- Enter the site from the west, which was likely the ancient access point. You will be in a shaded area near a bronze bust of Evans. Nearby are the kouloures, 15-foot-deep pits. At the very bottom of these pits, you can see Neolithic walls dating to approximately 7000 B.C.

- These *kouloures* demonstrate how Knossos is unusual for a Greek or European archaeological site; it is more like the Near Eastern sites called tells, where civilization after civilization built on the remains of the people who preceded them, layer upon layer.

- Now go west from the entrance, looping around the southern part of the palace. Go up the ramps and stairs to the high area that overlooks the central court.

- Be aware that the surrounding walls are a mix of genuine ancient walls and Evans's concrete reconstructions. Many of the frescoes, too, are replicas. While Evans based his work on genuine artifacts, especially the images found in those frescoes, many archaeologists have concerns about his work.

- The lower levels—the work rooms and storage rooms—were in considerably better shape than the upper royal living quarters of the palace. Evans was less conservative in his reconstructions than other archaeologists might have been, so the visitor needs to view these rooms with a skeptical eye.

- Ascend into Evans's reconstructed grand reception rooms. Bright and airy, they are very different from the grim enclosed architecture of much of the Mediterranean world. Note the fresco showing men and women seated as if spectators at a show. It was unusual in the ancient Mediterranean world for such gatherings not to be gender segregated.

- From the windows, you can look out over the countryside and the labyrinth of rooms beneath you. Here for the first time, the visitor can view the main feature of Knossos—the central courtyard—as an architectural unit. This is where the ancient bull dances may have been performed.

- Descend again into the central courtyard and look carefully for the overhang that conceals the so-called throne room. It is easy to miss. Visitors cannot enter the room, but they can peer inside.

- Evans was thrilled to find what he thought was a throne room here because it seemed to confirm the connection to Minos. However, this space is low and dark even with all its doors open and the morning sun shining in, and the supposed throne does not face the entranceway.

- Even the glorious griffins painted on either side of the throne does not keep this room from feeling more like a private meeting room than a public reception area for a monarch. In a way, this room is the single most mysterious area at Knossos.

- Back in the courtyard, we see demonstrated the Minoans' love of open air, light, and freshness they brought into their buildings. They could not only see the sky, but they could easily see the summits of the surrounding hills and mountains over their rooftops.

Linear A and Linear B

At least two forms of writing, known as Linear A and Linear B, were used throughout ancient Crete. Linear A is the older, used during the first and second palatial periods, while Linear B is from the third period, the period of Mycenaean rule.

For decades after they were discovered, these writing systems remained undeciphered. Then in the 1930s, a teenaged genius named Michael Ventris heard about the mystery and made decoding the scripts his life's work. With no formal training in archaeology or linguistics, he managed to crack the code of Linear B in 1952, proving it was a written form of Mycenaean Greek. Sadly, he was killed in a car crash a few years later, before he could solve the puzzle of Linear A.

Thus the language of the ancient Minoan kings and palace builders remains shrouded in mystery. One thing linguists are sure of: It is not a form of Greek.

- At the same time, this building gave its owners and inhabitants opportunities all over the palace to present themselves in a glorious and grand fashion on the colonnaded balconies and wide well-lit stairwells, as if they were on a stage.

- The whole building seems to be laid out for shows and displays. This would indicate not only a love of finery and appearances but also a strong element of social stratification in Minoan culture.

- On the east side of the courtyard, we find a range of rooms across several floors that Evans called the Queen's Quarters. They are beautifully decorated with frescoes, although the rosettes and dolphins you see there today were painted there at different times on different layers of plaster.

- Evans's name for these apartments was pure conjecture. All the Minoans seem to have lived in great grandeur, as indicated, for example, by the number of freestanding bathtubs scattered around the site, and by how every element of the palace, from those tubs to the cups and bowls and walls and floors, was lavishly decorated.

- In this same eastern part of the palace, a valuable set of discoveries was made about the working system that kept this great palace culture afloat. One was a set of jewelers' tools, which shows that this palace was also a center of work. The other was a set of clay tablets with writing on them.

- The latter clue was more remarkable because it was only the second indication we had that the preclassical Greeks were a literate society. The first was in the story of Bellerophon, the hero of Corinth and rider of Pegasus who carried stone tablets that might have had written messages on them.

- Imagine the amazement of Evans and his field director, archaeologist Duncan Mackenzie, when they found whole rooms that seemed to be dedicated to producing tablets written in Linear B. There were also much older areas of the palace that yielded Linear A tablets.

- Evans did not live to see the tablets deciphered, but amateur linguist Michael Ventris's work on Linear B eventually confirmed the Mycenaean conquest of Greece. He showed that Homer was right to say that during the time of the Trojan War (c. 1200 B.C.), a Mycenaean king ruled Knossos.

- More importantly, Ventris was able to show that the tablets were not the palace historical or diplomatic archive but simply its account books. This was evidence of a sort of bureaucratic system no one had dreamed existed in the ancient world.

- On the east side of the palace, take a look at the grand balcony with the traditional Minoan columns that converge on narrow bases and the image behind them of a charging bull. He's not in a courtyard nor surrounded by dancers, at least in the preserved part of this beautiful fresco. He is charging in a landscape with what might be a sacred tree behind him, his enormous horns about to gore whoever or whatever has attracted his notice.

- He is the best argument for seeing Knossos twice, because he is best visited in the morning, with the brilliant east sun shining on this masterpiece, this symbol that came to represent the royal house of Crete.

- As you end your tour, you will come down into the northern part of the palace to some broad ceremonial steps similar to those at Phaistos. In fact, they are so broad they seem less like steps than like a viewing platform or grandstand. It has been estimated that up to 500 people could have stood here to watch whatever was brought along the processional way below.

The Dodecanese—Kos, Patmos, and Rhodes

Lecture 15

The Dodecanese comprise 12 islands in the southeastern corner of the Aegean Sea. Among these fabulous islands, Kos, Patmos, and Rhodes have a special appeal. Kos is the eastern terminus of the Aegean arch of volcanism of which Santorini and Milos are such spectacular members, and that is where we will start.

- Kos was once home to a man whose ideas affect modern science to this day: Hippocrates.

- In the center of the modern town (also called Kos) is the old agora, where philosophers once stood before a great tree to discourse with their disciples.

- The plane tree standing here today, unfortunately, could not be the one where Hippocrates asked his students to swear their oath; it is not old enough. Still, it is one of the oldest trees in Europe, measuring about 45 feet in circumference at its base.

- A plaque near that tree displays the original form of the Hippocratic oath: "I swear by Apollo the healer, by Aesculapius and Hygeia and Panacea and all the gods and goddesses that, according to my ability and judgment, I will keep this oath."

- There follow many clauses about loyalty to the teacher and support of the teacher's sons because doctors at that time were a guild, then the ethics of dealing with patients, and then finally the closing: "While I continue to keep this oath unviolated, may it be granted to me to enjoy life and the practice of the art respected by all men in all times."

- Hippocrates as a boy would have gone to the Sanctuary of Apollo to practice his art, so we will go there now. It is about two and a half miles out into the countryside from the modern town of Kos.

- Although it was Apollo's sanctuary in Hippocrates's day, soon after his death it was rededicated to the healing god Aesculapius. This place was chosen as a spot for medical treatment because of its mineral springs, which are not uncommon in the Aegean.

Hippocrates, history's first scientifically minded physician, is Kos's most famous son.

- In ancient times, the lower terrace was covered with small enclosures in which people would receive special treatments or consultations.

- There are also some subterranean chambers on this level that have been identified as places of worship of Aphrodite.

- From the hilltop above the sanctuary, you can look out through the pine forest on a clear day and see the distant city of Bodrum, ancient Halicarnassus, on the Turkish coast. The Aphrodite worshiped here may in fact be the great mother goddess of Asia in disguise.

- Let's dispel the false notion that Aphrodite is being worshiped here as Venus, presiding over those stricken with venereal disease— diseases of erotic love. In ancient times, there were no venereal diseases. They are a recent development in human history.

- Among the discoveries on this lower terrace were tablets containing descriptions of cures. This is an extension of Hippocrates's idea of keeping careful records for future doctors' use.

- On the second terrace shows the religious aspect of this shrine. Immediately in front of you is a large altar on which visitors offered sacrifices on their own behalf. The skins of sacrificed animals were brought to the third level for a special purpose.

- Ascending to the third terrace, you will find something that links this site to other sites dedicated to Aesculapius and healing around the Greek world: sleeping chambers, where the sick would hope for dream visitations by the god. Here, they slept on the skins of those animals sacrificed below.

- The generally poor condition of this site is due to two factors. First, it was badly damaged in an earthquake in A.D. 522. Second, when the Knights of St. John arrived on this island, they used the fallen stones as a quarry to build their castle. (More on those knights later.)

- Around A.D. 95, during the reign of the Roman emperor Domitian, it was a custom of the Roman governors of Asia Minor to try to suppress conversion of their subjects to Christianity, because the Jews and Christians refused to worship the emperor as a god.

- One Christian man was exiled to the island of Patmos, quite a gentle treatment for his treason and rabble-rousing. We know this man as Saint John the Divine, author of the book of Revelation.

- A thousand years after John's time, a Byzantine monk named Christodoulos got permission from the Byzantine emperor to go to Patmos and build a monastery close to the spot where he believed John had had his vision. That is our next stop.

- Christodoulos believed John received his vision in a cave in the mountainous southern half of this hourglass-shaped island. When you visit the site today, you will see the cave is surrounded by the remains of an old nunnery.

- The cave is actually inside the chapel, on the right-hand side. It is very shallow, a sort of rocky shelter. A circle of silver laid into the stone is said to be the spot where John laid his head as he received his vision.

- Three strange grooves in the rock are said to be either a representation of the holy trinity or splits made by the voice sounding like a trumpet that spoke to John.

- The fame of this spot drew to the island many people who wanted to become monks, and for them, Christodoulos started a monastery higher up the mountain. This island was in a dangerous location, subject to raids by Saracen pirates during the Middle Ages, so the monks built their monastery in the form of a fortress.

- Around the monastery's courtyard, under the arcades, we see fragments of beautiful Byzantine frescoes as well as many spolia—objects taken from classical ruins such as mismatched columns, bits and pieces of doorways, and so forth put to new service in this monastery.

- Our third destination is Rhodes. As we enter the harbor, we see pillars on either side topped by Renaissance-era bronze statues, one of a stag, one of a doe. You may be told that these pillars once supported the feet of the Colossus of Rhodes. In fact, that wonder of the ancient world stood on one side of the harbor; it did not straddle it.

- The Colossus was a figure of the god Helios erected in about 280 B.C. He stood about 110 feet tall—10 feet shorter than the Statue of Liberty. He was crowned with the rays of the sun. Likely he stood with his legs close together, mounted on a marble pedestal that added 50 feet to his height. He was not a lighthouse but was a daytime landmark from far at sea.

- The Colossus was built as a victory monument after the people of Rhodes defeated one of the would-be successors of Alexander the Great at sea. The statue did not last very long, however. It toppled about 50 or 60 years later in one of the region's frequent earthquakes.

Hippocrates

Hippocrates is believed to have been born on the island of Kos around the year 460 B.C., shortly after the Persian Wars. He lived in the age of Herodotus, the classical age of Athens and its great naval empire.

Hippocrates lived a long life, possibly more than 80 years, and died not at home but in northern Greece sometime in the middle of the 4th century. Within a few decades of his death, the Kos islanders were inspired to make the gigantic sanctuary to Aesculapius because of the fame and glory Hippocrates had brought to the island.

Hippocrates believed that every set of symptoms needed to be carefully observed and recorded, a revolution he brought to medicine. As you can see from his original oath, he did not deny that gods were the source of healing, but he did add the elements of observation of symptoms and recording treatments and results to the practice of medicine. He is also important to the history of medicine because he instilled in his disciples the belief that prevention is the best cure.

Hippocrates was also interested in the effects of diet on health, and he (or one of his disciples) wrote a treatise with the evocative title, *Airs, Waters, Places* about how the land you are living in, the air you are breathing, the water you drink can have an effect on your health. It all sounds very modern, as does so much of Hippocrates's thinking.

- Look across the harbor mouth to see the Fortress of St. Nicholas, the patron saint of seafarers. This tower surrounded by a large wall is rounded to better withstand artillery fire.

- It was built by the Knights of St. John, also known as the Hospitallers. This order of monks was founded to serve pilgrims who became sick on their way to Jerusalem. They built the first of their great hospitals here on Rhodes. It lies at the foot of the Street of Knights.

- When the Crusades began, a military branch was added to the Hospitaller order. These were knights fighting for Christ, but they took the same vows of chastity, poverty, and obedience as the monks.

- As you ascend the Street of Knights, take time to look on either side at the different inns—the headquarters of the different groups of the Knights of St. John, which were based on the territory of their birth. Each section of the city's bastions was assigned to a different group. You will see national coats of arms (such as the French fleur-de-lis) as well as individual knights' coats of arms.

- The tourist route runs up the hill to the Palace of the Grand Masters. The towers on either side of the arched gateway still are original, but the rest is a reconstruction; the original castle blew up in the 1850s in a gunpowder accident.

- The Knights of St. John held out against the Byzantines and the Ottomans for over 200 years, but in 1522, Suleiman the Magnificent and his Janissaries captured this fortress. The knights negotiated a settlement and were able to take their men and their treasures to Malta, where they still exist in some form today.

- Our last destination on Rhodes is 35 miles south of the main harbor, the lovely little town of Lindos. Spend a night in one of the old houses there, some of which date back to the time of the Knights of St. John.

- Early in the morning, climb the hundreds of steps to the old acropolis of Lindos. Near the summit, you will see the stern of a ship carved into the hill. This is the best representation we have of a Hellenistic warship. It was originally part of the base of a heroic statue.

- Continue up the steps, and you will suddenly find yourself surrounded by dark walls. This was a fortress of the Knights of St. John. Further up, you will find their hall and the remains of their basilica church.

- At the top of the old acropolis rock, which has been used almost since prehistoric times as a place of worship and refuge, is a shrine of Athena—Athena Lindia. You can see some of the columns of her temple, then walk to the parapet, look out to sea, and see the Harbor of St. Paul, so called because it is believed he once landed there.

Welcome to Turkey—The Turquoise Coast
Lecture 16

If someone were to ask me where in the world you can find the most perfect blend of the beauties of nature, the glories of history, and the delights of travel, I would say without hesitation the Turquoise Coast of Southern Turkey. This stretch of coast, with its bays, cliffs, and tiny islands; deep blue waters; and golden sandy beaches reaches all the way from the city of Bodrum in the west to Antalya in the east on the big, notchlike bay in the center of Turkey's Mediterranean coast.

- Bodrum and Antalya bookend a fabulous chain of destinations: rivers, islands, monasteries, classical cities, lighthouses, rock-cut tombs, and sunken cities.

- There are three ways you can travel the Turkish coast: driving, hiking, and sailing.

  ○ The car route frequently takes you away from the sea, but there are still lots of wonderful stretches along the coast.

  ○ The hiking trail is a relatively recent innovation, put together from a series of existing goat tracks, foot paths, Roman roads, and lines along which Alexander the Great marched. It is not unlike America's Appalachian Trail, except this path seeks civilization as frequently as possible and brings you into contact with places to spend the night or have a meal.

  ○ The gulets, or two-masted schooners, you can rent for the journey offer unparalleled opportunities like anchoring in little coves overnight and climbing cliffs on otherwise inaccessible islands. The sail between Bodrum and Antalya takes about a week and can be very idyllic or claustrophobic, depending on what you are used to. Do your research carefully if you choose this option.

- Antalya is a wonderful city in its own right. Spreading out from the city along the shore in either direction are fabulous resorts. Within the city, the old Turkish quarter by the water is lined with houses and towering minarets.

- Bodrum was once known as Halicarnassus. In ancient times, it was home to the father of history, Herodotus, who lived in the 5th century B.C. Most of what we know about the Persian Wars comes from Herodotus and his insistence on eyewitness testimony.

- When the Greeks came across the sea from mainland Greece and created Halicarnassus, they blended to some extent with a local people called Carians, who gave the Greeks the crested helmet and the idea of a hand strap on the shield.

- Early on, Carians and Greeks fought together as mercenary armies as far away as Egypt.

© Hemera/Thinkstock.

Resorts line Antalya's harbor. To see its history, you must travel along the coast.

- Several generations later, a local dynast named Mausolus married his sister Artemesia, a queen of Halicarnassus. He was a general in the service of the Persian king of kings.

- Mausolus's death is an epic event in the history of architecture because the tomb that he and his wife planned for themselves, on the slope above the harbor in Bodrum, gave many future imitators its name. It is called the Mausoleum of Halicarnassus.

- Completed in the mid-4th century B.C., the tomb's design combined elements of a Greek temple, a victory monument, and a pyramid into a single overpowering block of stone ornamented with spectacular sculptures. A small off-center chamber deep inside contained the bodies of the king and queen and, presumably, many of their treasures.

- Nothing can be seen of it today. It was not only damaged by earthquakes, but its stones were taken away by medieval Crusaders in service of their castle building. Nonetheless, you can visit the spot where it once stood and a gallery that includes fragments of its sculpture.

- The not-to-be-missed site in Bodrum is the Castle of St. John, which is now a museum of discoveries from shipwrecks and nautical and underwater archaeology.

- The Turquoise Coast is the richest hunting ground in the world for important historic shipwrecks. In fact, the single most important shipwreck ever discovered, the Uluburun wreck, was excavated here in the 1980s under the direction of Cemal Pulak.

- This wreck dates to the about 1305 B.C., before the time of the Trojan War. It was a ship sailing from Canaan or Syria filled with treasures from Egypt and the Near East as well as a mass of tin and copper—the makings for bronze—all headed for Greece. Artifacts from some 11 different civilizations, from Sicily to the Balkans to the Near East, were onboard.

- There are some popular destinations close to Bodrum, like Cnidus, a city sacred to Aphrodite. One of the most famous statues in antiquity, Praxiteles's nude of Aphrodite, once stood in the temple here.

- As you go along the coast from west to east, you will pass from the land of the Carians to the land of the Lykians. They were a fascinating people with a league of a few dozen cities and a capital at Patara.

- The Lykians built extraordinary tomb monuments with high vaulted lids you can see on the inaccessible crags along your route. Almost all of these have been tipped over and broken into for their treasures.

- Other Lykian tombs were carved into flat cliffs and given facades like houses or temples, with triangular gables and small doors.

- Among the highlights of the Turquoise Coast are the snorkeling opportunities. No matter how you are traveling, you will want to get into the water. You will see sponges, corals, and fish of all kinds. If you are really lucky, you will see some of the world's last loggerhead turtles making for the beaches where they still lay their eggs.

- There are sunken cities, too, such as Kekova. A three-hour cruise from the little fishing village of Kas will take you to this underwater site, a sound between an island and the main coast.

- Kekova was sunken by an earthquake that left many of its walls and staircases standing. The best overview of Kekova, from outside the water at least, is from the castle tower on the acropolis.

- The Saklikent Gorge, near the lovely seaside city of Fethiye, is a little like the Samaria Gorge in Crete but even narrower and more tortuous. It is a naturalist's paradise, and you can also go tubing or rafting down the river.

- The "lost" city of Kaunos is best approached by sea if you can to a landing at Turtle Beach. Turtle Beach is the last nesting place of the loggerhead turtle (*Caretta caretta*), an animal on the verge of extinction.

- Head upriver from Turtle Beach through vast, tall reed beds full of wildlife. You will begin to see a distant mountainous crag with a castle on top—Kaunos.

- The ruins of Kaunos are a 10-minute walk from the nearest boat landing. They contain a spectacular theater, a citadel, baths, gymnasiums, agoras, stoas, even a Christian church with mosaics.

- Look across the reed beds to the distant cliff face to see the tombs of the lords of Kaunos. Archaeologists have found dishes inside these tombs, and we now understand that these were not just tombs but places where the dead were remembered with feasts.

- Continue upriver past the town of Dalyan to visit of the most famous mud baths in Turkey. The mud here contains sulfur, giving it some unique medicinal properties.

- Going east along the coast from Turtle Beach and Kaunos, you will suddenly come upon a wondrous strand of 11 miles of golden beach and turbulent water at Patara.

- Patara's ancient lighthouse was recently rediscovered and is being reconstructed by the Turkish Archaeological Service. It is a circular tower of great blocks of stone built in the time of the Roman emperor Nero.

- Further inland, you will find the bouleuterion, the old council house, where the governing body of the Lykian League met. Alexander Hamilton paid tribute to the league in the Federalist Papers.

- Unfortunately, we do not know the birthplace of Patara's most famous citizen, Saint Nicholas, or Santa Claus. But you will see plenty of signs in the neighborhood that refer to "Baba Noel."

- Pushing further east, you will come to Olympos—not to be confused with the Mount Olympus of the Greek gods. You can climb this active volcano and see the sacred flames where the Chimera was born for yourself.

- Down at the foot of the mountain is a lovely little river that was originally a broad channel allowing access for traders and pirates. Nearby is the tomb of a treasure hunter named Captain Eudemos bearing perhaps one of the most moving inscriptions you will read on your Aegean voyages:

  > The ship sailed into the last harbor and cast anchor to voyage no more. No longer was there hope for wind or sun, the light had faded. Captain Eudemos and his ship now rest after a life short as a day like a broken wave.

Central Turkey—Ankara, Konya, Cappadocia
Lecture 17

The highlands of central Turkey are home to great cities like Ankara and Konya and a marvelous region unlike any other part of earth, a place known as Cappadocia. The highlands were once home to one of the world's most popular poets, the 13th-century Sufi mystic Rūmī, and we will consider his life and work as we explore this world he knew so well. But first we visit Ankara, which became the capital of the modern Turkish republic after the fall of the Ottoman Empire.

- Istanbul, from time out of mind, had been the great city in this part of the world, but Turkey's first president, Kemal Ataturk, decided the capital should be in the heartland of Turkey.

- We can get to Ankara from Istanbul with a long drive or a short flight. The city is home to about 4 million people. A bustling place, it has a feel not unlike Washington DC, full of administrators and government officials.

- For the most part it is a new city. It expanded exponentially when it was chosen to be the capital, and it is marked with some remarkable monuments, such as Ataturk's mausoleum, created in the late 1940s, and the touching museum to the first president nearby.

- Ankara may have seemed an arbitrary choice, but in fact this is a region of ancient capitals. In the hills nearby, Hittite kings once ruled their empire from Hattusas among Cyclopean masonry, huge gates, statues of warrior kings, and rows of Hittite gods.

- We can fortunately read the writing of the Hittites because early on in Hittite history they adopted cuneiform from Assyrian traders. In the 19th century, linguists realized that Hittite was a lost member of the Indo-European language family.

- In addition to all this royal architecture, you can see the homes of the common people at Hattusas. You may be reminded of Tiryns and Mycenae, with which Hattusas is roughly contemporary.

- The Museum of Anatolian Civilizations in Ankara holds many wonderful artifacts from this site. The word "Anatolia" ("place where the sun rises") refers to the Turkish landmass, also called Asia Minor.

- Anatolian cultures go back thousands of years. Perhaps the most extraordinary treasures of the museum are from Çatal Hüyük, a site in central Turkey dating to about 9000 B.C. and first excavated in the 1960s by British archaeologist James Mellaart.

- Çatal Hüyük lies 28 miles outside our second great city, Konya, which was the adopted home of the poet Rūmī. Born in Tajikistan and raised speaking Persian, he and his family moved westward to "Rum"—that is, the former Roman Empire—from from which he later took his pen name.

- Rūmī was raised as a Sufi Muslim and trained as an expert on Islamic law. But he had a life-changing experience when he met a mystic named Shams and became his disciple and friend. He began to seek meaning in life outside the holy texts and in personal inspiration.

- Rūmī had a poetic gift like few others. Even today books of his poems sell millions of copies, even in translation.

- He wrote a poem about lost friendship after Shams's mysterious disappearance. For some time, Rūmī devoted his life to finding his lost master, then realized, "He and I are one. His spirit speaks through me. I have only been seeking myself."

- Rūmī's museum in Konya is his mausoleum. It is filled with memorials to his life and teaching. It also has a beautiful display of the musical instruments used in the ecstatic dances of the Sufi mystics that evolved into the tradition of the whirling dervish.

- The museum also reminds us of Rūmī's moving words on the nature of death: "When we die, do not look for our tomb in the Earth; seek it instead in human hearts."

- After Rūmī's death, his mausoleum became a center for study and reverence, where the Sufi mystical tradition is kept strong. There is an annual gathering of whirling dervishes from all over Turkey here each winter.

- Many people are drawn to central Turkey to see one of world's most extraordinary geologic formations in Cappadocia, "the land of horses."

- Millions of years ago, three big volcanoes spewed 300 feet of ash and lava over this landscape. This volcanic material was gradually compacted down to a volcanic stone called tuff.

- The volcanoes then began to spew basalt, which spread out over the tuff. The result was surface that looked quite stable, but then rain began to carve gullies in the basalt.

- Next, water from the summer rains froze in the hard snowy winters. It expanded, breaking that cap even further. Little by little, the underlying tuff was exposed to daylight again.

- The now-melted water rushed around in these new gullies, shaping cones and pillars in the tuff with basalt caps on top. The results were the famous fairy chimneys of Cappadocia.

- Ancient peoples were drawn to Cappadocia because it was high-quality grazing land. Volcanic soil is also very good for grapes and grains. There is still a wine industry here.

- Cappadocia became an important province of the Roman Empire under Emperor Tiberius. It developed lots of population centers during the early Christian period. Many different cultures met here, as did many armies.

- As early as the 7th or 8th century B.C., people lived in caves here, because the tuff was so easy to dig versus building a home out in the open.

- Two kinds of cave dwellers—troglodytes—emerged in this Cappadocian region. In the later period, Christian monks and nuns created communities of manmade caves by burrowing into a cliff face.

- Two of the best of these monasteries in existence are Göreme and Zelve, both protected UNESCO World Heritage Sites. They consist of halls, dwelling places, and chapels painted with frescoes.

- These communities may have been founded in secret when it was still illegal to be a Christian in the Roman Empire.

- Even more remarkable is a recent discovery of troglodytes who dug downward, rather than horizontally. It began with explorations of old wells and underground farmyard storage spaces.

- Archaeologists soon discovered hidden cities under the landscape of Cappadocia, almost 40 of them. Only a few have been opened, excavated, and explored.

- It is clear from the artifacts found in them that they were used by hidden Christian communities; whether the Christians were just using the caves carved out by earlier civilizations in Cappadocia or dug them themselves we do not know.

- We do know that there is nothing else in the world that equals the complexity and the scale of these sunken cities. The two most famous are Derinkuyu and Kaymakli.

- Typically there are round doors like the doors of fortresses; they are huge round millstones set in grooves so they can be rolled open and closed but no battering ram can knock them in. Those doorways are evidence that these are cities of refuge.

Çatal Hüyük

The word "Çatal Hüyük" (also spelled "Çatalhöyük") means "forked mound." When James Mellaart looked at this double tell (a "tell" being a layered manmade hill, a sure sign of ancient human occupation in the Middle East), he expected to find evidence of human habitation. But he never dreamed he would find one of the earliest examples of a complex human society.

The houses and buildings of Çatal Hüyük are unusual in that they do not open onto a grid of streets; rather, people reached the outside world by climbing ladders to holes in the roofs that opened onto terraced rooftops.

Among the extraordinary findings at Çatal Hüyük was the fact that complex religious and artistic traditions already existed at the dawn of civilization. Mellaart found an extraordinary figurine of what he believed was a mother goddess: a powerful looking woman with great sagging breasts and a protuberant or pregnant belly, seated on a throne that is decorated with leopards. Here is a powerful emblem of the mistress of beasts.

This figurine was found in a grain bin, but nonetheless when he coupled this figure with frescoes and other art he found, he realized that there was a huge cult of worship at Çatal Hüyük, as well as an elaborate cult of the dead. Skeletons at the site were found not in separate graveyards but in the floors of the houses. Human heads were kept in the living spaces, as if honored ancestors could be present in this way in the daily life of their descendents.

- Archaeologists and historians estimate that tens of thousands of people may have lived among these 40 or so underground cities on at least eight levels, possibly more.

- Each underground city was a warren of rooms. Every wall is stone. Each level has ventilator shafts to the surface. On the surface, those shafts are usually difficult to spot, so it is not likely that an enemy passing through would be able to locate them or block them up.

- There were stables underground for the livestock; wine presses; and vast storage areas for water, meat, and cheese. There were individual rooms for people or families, great meeting halls and workrooms, and wells.

- Archaeologically, underground cities are very hard to date. Nonetheless, they are a marvelous testimony to the power of human communal effort and shared vision.

- Both the cliff-face cities and underground cities are open to the public. They are worth visiting, because they allow us to put ourselves in the place of those whom fear had driven underground but whose ingenuity had also created such a remarkable solution to their predicament.

- As a final recommendation, no visit to Cappadocia is complete without a balloon ride over this extraordinary landscape. It is usually an early-morning excursion, but worth it.

Up the Meander River—Priene to Pamukkale
Lecture 18

O ne of the best rivers in the world for a river cruise vacation lies in western Turkey—the Meander River, whose name is the etymological root of the English word meaning "to wander aimlessly." Along the way, you can take in the classical ruins bordering this once important artery.

- The ancient Greeks called this river Maiandros. It lies on a flat plain as it heads toward the sea, and it is wrapped in silt all along its length, so its course is sluggish and it forms an enormous delta at its mouth.

- There were many classical cities along the Meander, including Magnesia near its mouth, with its wonderful, now fallen, Temple of Artemis; Tralles, with its fantastic set of Roman water pipes; and Nysa, with its beautiful carved marble theater reliefs.

- We are going to focus on three fantastic cities: Priene, down near the mouth of the river; Aphrodisias, further up; and Pamukkale, the modern name for ancient Hierapolis, which is up in the hills.

- A recommended style of traveling the Meander for those who do not speak much or any Turkish is to hire a guide who can act as a driver and interpreter. Such a guide can not only take you to major sites but can speak to the locals about sites off the beaten tourist path.

- Priene is a spectacular and unusual site from the ancient world. Rather than being built and rebuilt over the centuries, it was planned and built all at once around 350 B.C., then abandoned before the Romans arrived.

- It is a time capsule with which we can view civic life of Greeks living in Asia in the centuries following the life of Alexander the Great.

- Priene sits on a crag 1,000 feet high on the north bank of the Meander River. The river was the city's lifeline, and when the harbor silted up, the city was abandoned.

- There had been an earlier Ionian Greek city called Priene further up the river that had also been silted up. Its refugees built this city with the financial support of Mausolus of Halicarnassus.

- This second Priene was laid out by one of the successors of Hippodamos of Miletus, the first city planner we know by name. Hippodamos's ideas survive in urban planning to this day: rectangular grids, wide main boulevards leading to smaller streets, easy access to civic and religious centers, and so on.

- It is good to go to Priene very early or very late in the day because the site faces due south and can be extremely hot in the summer. There is a 10- or 15-minute climb from the parking area to the site proper.

- Enter through the city gate and look to either side. You are looking at one of the best preserved and best built of all Hellenistic fortification walls. Mausolus spared no expense, and the result was a virtually impregnable city.

- The city is a place of extraordinary order. The main boulevards run straight ahead of you, east-west, following the contour line of the sloping cliff face. The north-south streets, which go down the slope, are much narrower and sometimes precipitous, even becoming staircases in certain places.

- You will also see careful arrangements of drains and scoring on the rocks to carry rainwater away.

- Straight ahead you will come to a remarkable building that was the council hall for all the male citizens of Priene. It is like a theater but square instead of semicircular. There is an altar, probably to the local civic deity, where the stage would normally be.

- The size of this building relative to the number of homes in Priene is a sign that this city was governed by a democratic assembly of all free adult male citizens.

- Further along, our way opens up into the great agora, with its many colonnades. From the edge of the agora, steeper streets lead down to the gymnasium and the stadium.

- Go uphill to visit the grand Temple of Athena. This temple has double interest for the visitor: the beauty of its still-standing ionic columns (designed by Pythias, who also designed the Mausoleum), and the fact that the temple's completion was funded by Alexander the Great.

- The temple's altar is very much in ruins, but to its north and east (that is, a bit left as you return toward the gate), you will come upon a miniature Christian basilica with several aisles and, in the middle, a lovely example of an ambo, a place for walking.

- The gem of Priene lies beyond this little church at the edge of the community, near the path up to the acropolis. One of the loveliest theaters in the entire Greco-Roman world is built into the hillside.

- The theater is small in scale, but its acoustics are perfect, and it has an unusual feature: a proskene, columns that supported an elevated stage that intruded into the performing area. This setup was associated with comedies involving stock characters and gags championed by a Greek playwright named Menander.

- On some of those columns, you can see the remains of the brilliant paint that decorated them 2,000 years ago.

The Temple of Athena at Priene is powerful evidence of Greek civilization's reach far into the Asian continent.

© Comstock Images/Getty Images/Thinkstock.

- The skene building here is also important for theater historians. It is one of the few places where the socket for the deux ex machina is still visible.

- Return to the river and wind upstream through beautiful modern Turkish towns with gleaming mosque domes until you reach a city that is almost pure Roman, Aphrodisias.

- As Priene was sacred to Athena, Aphrodisias was sacred to Aphrodite, the Roman Venus. Behind both of these female divinities may lie the mother goddess of Asia, who can be traced to the Neolithic mistress-of-beasts figurines. It appears that Greek colonists deliberately intertwined one of their goddesses with the local mother goddess when they arrived.

- Aphrodisias is one of the great ruined cities of the world, well worth a full day's visit. Outside a circle of walls two miles around, you will see the sarcophagi of hundreds of noble and wealthy families who lived here during the Roman Empire.

- This city was favored by the Romans because in 88 B.C., in the turmoil of late Roman Republic, Aphrodisias remained loyal despite its distance from Rome. You are witnessing the results of the largess of the grateful senators toward their loyal allies.

- Some of the most interesting sarcophagi are of the athletes and charioteers; one charioteer's sarcophagus shows every single wreath he ever won. It was also very common to show husbands and wives as household gods, their heads portrayed as busts.

- Inside Aphrodisias's walls, you will find an area so vast it is almost too much to take in, but here are some of the highlights.

  o The bathhouses near the enormous theater and the baths further on that were a gift from Emperor Hadrian are typified by great domes, some of which are almost complete. These domes, still a part of modern Turkish baths, served a practical purpose—letting cold condensation slide down the curves rather than drip on the bathers.

  o In the northern part of the city, the Sebasteion marks the site of emperor worship in the city. (The word comes from the Greek translation of the name Augustus, "Sebastos.") The ceremonial entryway, with its long colonnades, is well preserved; the hundreds of statues that once stood here are now in the site museum.

  o Aphrodisias has wonderful temples, especially the lovely Temple of Aphrodite. However, as elsewhere in the East, this temple was later adapted for Christian use. Its inner colonnade was removed to allow room for a large congregation.

- At the north end of the town is the most wonderful surviving stadium in the Roman world, perhaps even surpassing the Circus Maximus in Rome. The racing area is huge, about 800 by 200 feet, with room to seat 30,000 people. The race course is not a straight-sided oval but bulges in the middle, so that every attendee can get a good view of the action. Unusually, this stadium also hosted gladiatorial combats.

- Admire above all the unique, pale, blue-gray marble all over the site, seen most beautifully in the columns with spiral fluting. This wonderful marble comes from quarries in the mountains to the north and was exported all over the Mediterranean world.

- Our last stop along the Meander River is called Pamukkale today, a name that means "cotton castle." The ancients called this city at the top of a cliff Hierapolis, which means something like "holy city" or "city of shrines."

- This place is one of those wondrous marriages of a natural wonder with human creation. Hot springs bubble from the top of these sheer cliffs, bringing lots of sulfur and carbon dioxide to the surface.

- As these gasses and minerals bubbled out, they flowed across the surface of the cliff and slid down the precipice. The calcium in the water coated the cliff face, building up like stalactites and stalagmites in a cave.

- Little by little that cliff face was covered by a sheet of snow-white calcite. Then, as blocks of stone began to alter the water's flow, pools formed on the cliffs. The west-facing cliffs became a spot where one could bathe in natural hot springs as if floating in midair.

- As a result of this, ancient Hierapolis became a spa, one of those places the ancients sought out for its healing waters, and a city arose on the top of a cliff to serve them.

- Late in antiquity, as Rome faded away, Christianity took hold strongly in this city. The circular mausoleums found outside the town remind us of the classical Christian taboo against keeping the dead alongside the living.

- One particular mausoleum is of great interest to Christians, the Martyrium of St. Philip. The saint was said to have been stoned here in Hierapolis, and although his burial place is unknown, this elaborate square building, capped by a dome, commemorates his martyrdom.

- There was also a grand Temple of Apollo here with its own oracle cult. The temple was deliberately built over one of the vents through which the noxious gasses came up from below. There was a tradition that the god more or less claimed his own sacrifices when bulls or sparrows placed near the vent would die from inhaling the fumes.

- Recent ground-penetrating radar studies of the temple show that there are subterranean cavities and chambers underneath it. These still wait exploration. However, you can find the crack from which the vapors emerge at the west end of the temple, in a niche with an ornamented arch.

- End your visit to Pamukkale by going down to the edge of the cliff and joining the throngs of modern locals and visitors who bathe in these unique bubbling springs among Roman pillars that may mark the spot of a Roman bathhouse, pick a basin, and take your bath looking out over the Meander River from the face of the cliff itself.

A Wonder of the World—Ephesus

Lecture 19

The most beautiful surviving facade from all of Greek and Roman history is made of golden, almost honey-colored stone. It is two stories high, and a broad flight of steps runs up to its several doorways, each with elaborately carved marble around them. Columns carry out pediments from the main wall of the facade, and niches hold the statues of four beautiful women. We are not in Rome. We are not in Athens. We are in Ephesus, gazing upon a library built by a son in memory of his father.

- Ephesus was the home of one of the Seven Wonders of the Ancient World, the great Temple of Artemis, as well as one of the seven churches of Asia to whom Saint John addressed the book of Revelation. It has ties to Christian, Roman, Greek, and shadowy pre-Greek Asian religions.

- Ephesus is a double city, although that may not be initially clear to a visitor. If you come by sea to the port of Kusadasi, a tour bus may bring you straight from the ship to an immense archaeological site. This is only one of the two places called Ephesus in ancient times.

- When the Greeks first came here around 1000 B.C., Ephesus occupied a central point in their stretch of 12 Ionian settlements. It was planted initially at the spot where Selçuk stands today. One lonely column at Selçuk marks the spot of the great Temple of Artemis. Other remains of the Greek colony are buried about 30 feet deep.

- In the time of the successors of Alexander the Great—that is, in the late 4th or early 3rd century B.C.—a great leader called Lysimachus moved the people of Ephesus to higher ground, closer to the harbor, which was continually receding from them as the local river silted it up. These are the ruins most tourists visit, which we will visit first.

- If you enter through the harbor gate, soon you will see the great theater, the site of a riot in which Saint Paul was almost killed by the silversmiths of Ephesus for his preaching against the cult of Artemis (Roman Diana). This is also the monumental part of the site.

- Many guides, however, prefer to take visitors through the uphill gate, the so-called Magnesia Gate, which led to the city of Magnesia near the Meander River.

- Inside the gates, you will come first to the State Agora. You may want to wander along the stoas, porticos, and passageways around the agora rather than the main boulevard, until you come the Prytaneion.

- The Prytaneion was the town hall. Adjoining it is a lovely banqueting hall where distinguished foreigners were treated to fine meals at the expense of the town and its counselors.

- As the street moves out of the public area, we see monuments associated with Roman emperors. On the left is a great stone and earth platform where once stood a temple erected by Emperor Domitian. The upper columns are caryatids—columns in human form—some representing barbarian peoples conquered by Rome.

- Drop back down onto the main road and admire the broad open airy spaces, noticing the statue bases interspersed among the columns. Everybody wanted to be commemorated in the Hellenistic and Roman world, and anybody who had a bit of money could put up a statue to themselves, an ancestor, or a god and give themselves credit as a donor on the pedestal.

- Nearby is the Temple of Hadrian, with a beautiful arch over its entryway and pedestal for statues outside its lovely colonnade.

- Looming on the left as you continue down the slope is a vast area covered by a modern translucent roof. This structure shelters a group of terrace houses called *insulae*, or islands. You have to go to Pompeii or Herculaneum to find anything as well preserved.

- The houses are built on three different terrace stages going up the hillside like stair steps. As a result, the lower levels have light wells, atriums, and colonnaded courts instead of windows to let in air and light. At the same time, the roof of one level served as a terrace for the occupants of the level above.

- Although there is an extra charge to visit these houses, I strongly recommend that you do so. Not only is it a model of how to display a complex archaeological site both safely and comprehensibly; the architecture and artifacts are truly wondrous, particularly the mosaics and frescoes being painstakingly preserved and restored by a joint Austrian-Turkish archaeological team.

- From above the terrace houses, you can see the crowds milling in front of the place where we began the lecture, the Library of Celsus. Go down and join the crowd for a closer look.

- There is a low area below the steps, which would have made the facade even more towering and impressive. To Ephesus's Roman citizens, this facade would have resembled a theater skene.

- In the early 2nd century A.D., the Roman proconsul of Asia was a man named Celsus. Ephesus was his unofficial capital. When he died, his son, who had loved him very much, decided to treat him as if he had been a classical hero, a semidivine being.

- The traditional thing to do for a classical hero was give him a grave monument where people could come and worship called a heroon, a place for the hero. That is what this library was in essence.

The Library of Celsus is not only beautiful, it is a son's moving memorial to his beloved, learned father.

- Celsus was entombed beneath the library and remembered there like a hero through learning, reflection, and philosophy, which says a lot about both father and son.

- The library was shaken down by an earthquake about 150 years after it was built, but part of the facade lasted into the Middle Ages. Enough fragments survived for the rest to be reconstructed more recently.

- The four female statues represent four qualities of the human character. From left to right they are Sophia (wisdom), Arete (excellence), Ennoia (judgment), and Episteme (expertise).

- Enter through the doors and you will find yourself in large, lofty rectangular hall. Although the facade was two stories, the interior was one room with two levels of galleries or balconies around the walls.

- The books were not rectangular codices with spines like our books. They were scrolls, most likely labeled with tags hanging off the ends, stacked in cubbyholes.

- We know from records of the ancient Library of Alexandria that the books were arranged by genre: comedies, tragedies, philosophy, technical manuals, histories, and so on. We do not know what happened to the scrolls that were kept here at Ephesus.

- Outside the library, there was a public latrine nearby. This facility could accommodate 40 users at a time and, unlike the modern equivalent, consisted of open spaces, not private cubicles. However, running water beneath the seats did wash away the waste.

- Across the streets from the library were the public baths and a brothel. Guides love to point out a place on the pavement where, not too far from here, a bare human foot and the head of a beautiful woman wearing a headdress are painted on the street, as if to say, "This way to the brothel!"

- Your guide may or may not suggest there was a tunnel that led under the street from the library to the brothel so that men could tell their wives they were going to the library when they were actually attending to less intellectual pursuits. There is no such tunnel. There would not have needed to be. There was no stigma attached to satisfying the needs of the body in the ancient Greek and Roman world.

- The single most impressive monument in the city is its theater, one of the largest and best preserved in the Greco-Roman world. It is still used for performances.

- Even when listening to more modern musical compositions performed here, you can hear how the acoustics favor double-reed instruments like oboes and the bassoons. The ancients had a pipe called an aulos, not unlike an oboe, that accompanied performances in these theaters.

- This is also the theater, as mentioned earlier, where Saint Paul was nearly killed in the silversmiths' riot while spreading religion of Christianity, because the exclusive nature of Christianity harmed the silversmiths' business.

- A large part of the silversmiths' business was making souvenir images of gods and heroes. A silversmith called Demetrios, when he heard Paul preaching that everything about the worship of Artemis of Ephesus was a sham and a fraud, started a chant: "Great is Diana of the Ephesians!"

- All the other silversmiths joined. Large parts of the population joined. Paul barely escaped with his life. The magistrates were called in and it became a court case.

- From the theater, you can also look down the beautiful straight road to the old harbor, but there's no harbor there anymore. The ruthless river filled up the bay over the centuries. The open sea now lies far away.

- The walk down to the gate takes us past another monument, though few people bother to explore it: the gymnasium and the sporting area, with its small gladiatorial stadium. Archaeologists have recently uncovered a gladiators' cemetery near here.

- Back in the museum in Selçuk, you can see X-rays of these gladiators' skeletons. They were big, brawny professional fighters marked horribly by wounds and injuries from a wide array of horrific weapons.

- Here in Selçuk, a remarkable little town in its own right, climb the hill, which was the citadel of the old city of Ephesus. There you will find a great Christian basilica dedicated to Saint John—although which Saint John is not clear.

- Tradition suggests that Saint John the Apostle took Mary, the mother of Jesus, to Ephesus after Jesus's death and resurrection, and that she lived out her days there. There is an extensive and ancient cult to Mary in this area.

- Once you have explored the basilica, walk away from the altar to the western terrace. You can see the single column of the Temple of Artemis below. It was discovered by archaeologists that there have been numerous temples on that site.

- The temple of the classical period was famous for having burned down on the day Alexander the Great was born. The column you see is from the famous Great Wonder that followed that, but it was destroyed in an earthquake. Its stones were carried away to form parts of other buildings, including Hagia Sophia in Istanbul.

- The goddess who presided there, Artemis, would be very mysterious to us except for a remarkable find. Carefully buried at Ephesus was a statue of the original Artemis, apparently interred by her worshipers to keep her safe from vengeful iconoclastic Christians.

- The statue has the face of a young girl, crowned with a huge headdress decorated with beasts. She wears a breastplate covered with what may be eggs, breasts, or bull's testicles. Whatever they are, she is no maiden huntress of the classical Greek religion. She is something new to us, a fusion of the Greek Artemis with that Asian mistress of beasts, perhaps.

- End your day in Selçuk. In winter, you may be able to enjoy that unique sport of camel wrestling. At almost any time of the year, you can enjoy the fountains and monuments of the city's squares, as well as its restaurants.

- The great arches of a Roman aqueduct march along the city's north side, and each broken arch may be crowned with the nest of a stork. I hope that the end of your time in Ephesus will be not a yearning in nostalgia for past glories, but a feeling that even in the most ancient and broken of ruins new life still goes on.

Royal Cities of Asia—Pergamon and Sardis
Lecture 20

Turkey has within its borders the remains of many ancient kingdoms. In fact, the landmass we call Anatolia or Asia Minor was a laboratory for the idea of empire. We will visit Sardis, the capital of ancient Lydia, and Pergamon, the capital of a great empire of Attalid kings, successors of Alexander, who ultimately ruled over much of what is today modern Turkey.

- Most visitors' jumping-off point for both ancient cities is likely the great modern city of Izmir, built on the ancient remains of the Greek colony of Smyrna. Smyrna is one of several places that claims to be the home city of the poet Homer.

- Izmir has a great airport that can be easily reached from Istanbul and a wonderful harbor that can bring you here from various points in the Mediterranean. However you choose to arrive, I urge you to use Izmir as your base for touring Pergamon, Sardis, Ephesus, and Izmir itself.

- Long ago, central and western Asia Minor were home to the kingdom of the Lydians. By the time the Greeks arrived, late in their history, they had been wealthy conquerors for many generations and had become soft pleasure seekers who hired Greek hoplites to do their fighting for them.

- We have to imagine, then, a time when they were ruthless conquerors who took a small area around the Pactolus River in highlands near the Aegean coast and expanded into an empire from the Black Sea in the north to the Mediterranean in the south, including virtually all of the Aegean coast of Turkey.

- The kings who ruled from Sardis were supreme. They had one king, Croesus, whose name became synonymous with wealth. The Greeks credited him with inventing money—that is, the use of tokens for commerce rather than barter.

- Sardis lies on an upland plain where mountains along the south side of the Pactolus River frame a citadel on a foothill. On top of that citadel stood the palace of King Croesus and his ancestors, a place of unimaginable luxury.

- Their wealth was built on the flecks of gold and silver combined in a compound we call electrum found in the rocks of the surrounding mountains. The kings of Lydia decided at some point that this stuff had value, so a quantity of electrum would be collected, melted into a ball, and pressed into a coin.

- With this wealth, Sardis became one of the most fantastic royal citadels in Asia. Unfortunately, it was looted again and again. Virtually nothing remains of the court of King Croesus. His kingdom was conquered by King Cyrus of Persia, the first king of a rapidly expanding empire from further east.

- Although little is left of the citadel, parts of the city are visible to visitors, protected from the elements by a canopy. It can be confusing but is still worth a visit.

- What you will be struck by is the modesty of the houses relative to the city's famed wealth. They were apparently mostly of mud brick. These were probably the working-class residences, where people lived jammed up against the city's stone and earth ramparts.

- The walls confuse military scholars because they seem to have a ramp running up the outside, which would allow attackers up to the top. On the other hand, the bare ramp may have exposed attackers to archers on the walls better than ladders did.

- The city got a new lease on life in terms of its importance and grandeur in the time of the Hellenistic kings and later during the Roman Empire. At the foot of the hill is an enormous Ionic temple once dedicated to Artemis. Its two immense remaining columns frame the surrounding mountains beautifully.

- Clustered near the foot of the temple's columns are the remains of a Byzantine church made of ordinary brick. Its low dome contrasts with the grandeur and majesty of the columns of Artemis, yet it has better endured the centuries.

- Around the base of the citadel hill and across the highway, we find a cluster of Greco-Roman public buildings, including a gymnasium, a temple, a civic center, a theater, and baths.

- Before entering a bath, a Greek athlete would cover his skin in olive oil and use an implement called a strigil to scrape most of the dirt, sweat, and dead skin off the surface of his body. Thus the strigil became the emblem of Greco-Roman athletics.

The Romans left their stamp here, in the form of the Temple of Artemis, among other structures that cluster beneath the Lydian citadel.

- The gymnasium immediately adjoins the best preserved and most monumental synagogue of the early Jewish Diaspora. There was probably a community of Jews living at Sardis as early as the Hellenistic period, but it grew under the Roman emperors, and sometime in the late Roman or early Byzantine Empire, the synagogue was built on part of the old gymnasium grounds.

- This synagogue was unparalleled for spaciousness and decoration, particularly its mosaics, in the ancient Mediterranean world. Enter the building through its square, colonnaded courtyard with the central fountain that may have been used for ritual purification.

- Pass into the central area and admire the dazzling mosaic floors and beautiful marble-paneled walls, built with a technique called opus sectile.

- Notice the pedimented niches on either side. These are believed to have been the places where the scrolls of the Torah were kept. A ceremonial table would have stood at the far end and, behind that, a semicircular structure like a tiny theater called the synthronon is where the elders would have sat during rituals.

- On to Pergamon, created by Attalid kings who succeeded Alexander the Great as rulers of the Macedonian Greeks, generals and advisors during his conquest of Asia in the 330s and 320s B.C.

- Pergamon was built in the following century on a grand, high acropolis with a city at its foot, which is now the modern Turkish town of Bergama, where we start our explorations.

- Many of the remains in the lower town do not go all the way back the Attalid dynasty, descended from a Macedon ruler called Attalos, but one that does is the Asclepieion, a sanctuary of Aesculapius that resembles in its function the one at Epidauros or Kos.

- There are some unusual features in this Asclepieion; one is the use of circular rooms where the patients spent the night hoping for a dream from the god.

- An important medic from the Roman Empire named Galen was inspired to take up his trade by a visit here. Galen took over where Hippocrates left off, writing volumes of practical advice about anatomy and medicine. He seems to have spent some time as an army medic as well.

- On the lower level of the shrine, you will encounter the grand brick walls of the temple of the Egyptian god Serapis and inside it a Christian church dedicated to Saint John the Apostle.

- Do not leave the lower town without visiting the Museum of Pergamon because although its exhibitions are few, it has a scale model of the most important feature of High Pergamon, the royal citadel: the great altar of Zeus.

- On this altar were gigantic sculptural friezes, practically three-dimensional sculptures, depicting a battle between gods and giants, which was a metaphor for the battle between the kings of Pergamon and the Celtic Galatians—civilization versus barbarism.

- The site also contained a large, square space where sacrificial fires to the god Zeus burned, surrounded by these fantastic sculptures.

- The altar is on a terrace of its own apart from the rest of the high citadel. Because the altar is gone, most visitors do not go down to the terrace, so you may have to ask for directions. All that remains of the great altar is its square footprint and a few surrounding pine trees.

- Climb back up to the upper citadel and note how high above the city you are. There are no natural springs in this hill, so how did the ancients get water up to these heights?

- A hydraulics expert was brought in, who noticed that there were springs at a higher level than this acropolis on some nearby hills. Knowing that water seeks its own level, he piped the water in airtight tubes from those springs to the acropolis. You can see the remains of this amazing hydraulic system thanks to the archaeological excavations.

- You will also see one of the most impressive theaters in the ancient world here—impressive not for its size or acoustics but for the steepness of its seats.

- A number of temples exist on the acropolis. The most magnificent was the temple of the deified Roman emperor Trajan, built by his successor Hadrian.

- The last king of Pergamon had bequeathed his kingdom to Rome during the late Roman Republic, giving Rome a big foothold in Asia and making Rome forever grateful for this gift.

- You will also see humble traces of life in the high citadel. All the people serving the citadel and temples had to be fed, so in addition to that water system, you will find the remains of an understory of magazines and granaries.

- The kings of Pergamon were followers of Alexander the Great, who had loved learning as much as conquest. Thus the remains of Pergamon's acropolis also include a library.

- In fact, the kings of Pergamon were in a sort of knowledge arms race with Alexander's other successors, the Ptolemaic rulers of Egypt. At one point, the Egyptians became so envious of this vast center of learning that they put an embargo on sending papyrus to Pergamon.

- This embargo prompted experimentation with parchment. It was here at Pergamon that parchment first became part of the mainstream tradition of bookmaking.

- It is shocking to think that this city and everything it stood for fell under attack by John the Divine when he wrote the book of Revelation. One of the seven copies of the book was sent to the church at Pergamon, and the letter accompanying it said, "You live where Satan's throne is."

- What did Saint John mean? Why is Pergamon Satan's throne? Was it the cult of the emperor? The altar of Zeus? The knowledge of the ancients contained in the library? Looking at this beautiful place, it is hard to imagine it as evil. It seems more like paradise on earth.

Troy—Beyond Homer and the Trojan Horse
Lecture 21

Today we are joining Homer and his heroes at Troy, the setting of the *Iliad*, that epic story that has seized the imagination of millions through the ages. A visit to Troy can be the highlight of your time in Turkey, or it can be a confusing day wandering under an oppressive sun around a chaotic archaeological site; the goal of this lecture is to help avoid the latter and get the most out of your visit.

- Your likeliest approach to Troy is by crossing the Hellespont, the strait that separates Europe from Asia, by ferry. The ferry port of Çanakkale has a wonderful museum.

- You will also be greeted by a recognizable Trojan Horse, a prop from the 2004 Warner Bros. film *Troy*. Note that the horse does not appear in the *Iliad*, which covers only a short period at the end of the Trojan War, but is from an episode of the war recounted in the *Odyssey*.

- You will see another, less convincing replica Trojan Horse at the parking lot of the archaeological site of Troy itself. Pick up a map at the visitors' center before heading down the path to the observation level, where you can walk back and forth and view the site.

- You may have expected a great city with towering walls, gates, and monuments. Instead, it is a tell—one of those manmade layer cakes of settlements—topped by a jumble of mud brick.

- There are no fewer than 9 major phases of settlement and 50 individual strata, or layers, on this site. It is simultaneously an invaluable find and an archaeologist's nightmare. Some large artifacts, like sections of wall, start low (early) in the tell and reach high (late) in the tell, above later artifacts, making the site an archaeological jigsaw puzzle.

- When entering the site itself, the first object you encounter at ground level is more of that big, ancient wall. This square foundation for a stone tower demonstrates what a tremendously strong citadel this was.

- This is part of what archaeologists call Troy VI—that is, the sixth city of Troy counting upward from the bottom—built around 1700 B.C., in the middle to late Bronze Age, which lasted almost 500 years and was destroyed by fire around 1250 B.C.

- If the Trojan War recounted by Homer is on some level historical fact, then Troy VI is that Troy—the Troy of the *Iliad*.

- Turn right at the foot of the entry steps, follow the wall, and you will see a sort of corridor. Notice how different the masonry of the right-hand wall is. It is the retaining wall for a temple platform from

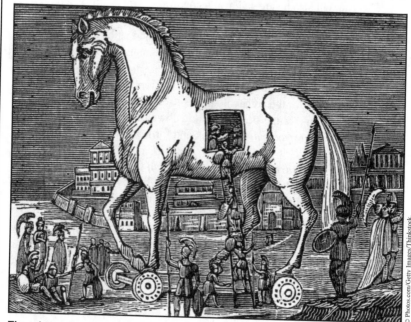

There is much more to Troy's history than the stories told in Homer's *Iliad*.

© Photos.com/Getty Images/Thinkstock.

more than 1,000 years later, late Greek or early Roman times. Once again, we see the problem of dating objects found at Troy when even huge walls can be jumbled.

- Follow the corridor to a gate into Troy VI. Notice the dogleg before the gate that was a sophisticated piece of ancient military technology. It functioned as a killing box, slowing approaching enemies so that soldiers on the walls could fire down on them, and it rendered battering rams useless—no room to maneuver one.

- Enter the citadel of Troy VI. Around you, especially to the left, are houses. Beyond these is a rectangular temple, with two rows of five round pillar bases. In the middle are two big circular stones, perhaps for massive pillars, or perhaps to hold figures of some kind.

- Next you will come to the inside face of the Troy VI wall you followed before to find a stout building of rough stone jammed between the temple and the wall, where excavators found many jars dating to the Troy VII period—between about 1250–1050 B.C.

- Around that time, the city fell to fire and assault, and this building is one of the city's adaptations for siege conditions—food and drink stored in every available nook.

- For now, retrace your steps back to the main path and continue north toward the small acropolis and the Temple of Athena dating to 700 B.C., built by Greeks who returned to this site after it had been abandoned for centuries. The returning Greek settlers renamed the city Ilium; Homer uses "Troy" and "Ilium" interchangeably in the *Iliad*.

- This Temple of Athena lasted down to the time of Alexander the Great, who came here in 334 B.C. on his Asian campaign. Later, Julius Caesar found the temple in disarray and had it restored, so we see a mix of Hellenistic and Roman material here.

- The podium of the temple is on one side and a tower on the other, inside which is a cistern. This is a reminder to us of a real weakness of Troy as a fortified site: The springs are all outside. Homer makes a point of this.

- The temple terrace also offers beautiful, panoramic views of the Hellespont to the north and a vast plain to the west which, geologically speaking, is a fairly recent development. In the time of the Trojan War, it was a bay, probably the harbor of Troy.

- Around the base of the temple mound are scattered remains of the temple's roof coffering. You will see little flowers carved in the marble in each one.

- So far, we have been in the Troy that was excavated in slow detail by British scholar and diplomat Frank Calvert, the first to identify this hill as Homer's Troy, in the 1860s.

- In the 1870s, a German millionaire named Heinrich Schliemann provided the money, manpower, and permits for massive excavations down to the tell's lowest foundations. The wall and gate you will come to next is part of that foundation—Troy I, dating to 2900 B.C.

- This wall tells us that even at the beginning, Troy was a fortified site. The people of Troy, judging from the pottery and material culture at the lowest levels, were a very different group of people from the dynasty of Priam 1,200 years later. Such a warlike culture was very unusual in Anatolia in this period.

- Continue beyond the gate of Troy I and look off to your right. The first remains are of the Megaron of Troy II. Schliemann thought this was a royal house from Homer's time, but he was 1,000 years off. In fact, to get to the "real" Troy, Schliemann bulldozed through his actual target, destroying it forever.

- Beyond that fragment of the Megaron, still on the right, there is a house from Troy I with beautiful herringbone masonry. Even simple houses here had touches of such delightful artistry.

- Before you is a different world again, the world of the modern excavations performed mostly by German archaeologists funded by Mercedes Benz, using modern techniques and modern care and analysis. Here you can see them at work by crossing the bridge over their excavations.

- Then you return to the world of Schliemann and another large gate from Troy II, a level of megaconstruction rivaling anything to be found in the Near East. This southwest-facing gate was once sheathed in copper or bronze and must have gleamed impressively in the strong sunlight.

- Go through the gate and turn right to find the most famous spot in all of Schliemann's digging, where he claims he found the Treasure of King Priam hidden beneath a tarnished copper pot. In truth, he probably assembled the treasure from all over the site or even bought some of the goods locally. Also, they date from Troy II, not Priam's era.

- At this point, you will have almost completed the east-west crossing of the tell and should be back out at the wall of Troy VI, with the wall of Troy II on your right. You will have to loop north and come back south to see two more important finds from Troy VI: in front of you, a fortified palace, and to the right, a blocked up gate.

- Tour guides are fond of saying this gate is the spot where the Greeks, in the dead of night, breached the walls of Troy, hauled in the Trojan Horse, and hastily patched up the walls again. A charming thought, but there is no evidence for or against the notion.

- The building ahead is what Schliemann called Priam's Palace. The structure itself dates to Troy VI, and during Troy VII—the time of the city's destruction—it was filled with storage jars as for a siege, so perhaps he was right.

- Take a right and exit the citadel over the wall of Troy VI. Outside, we are in a different world—Troy VIII and IX, the world of the later Greeks and the Romans, which the Romans called Ilium Novum, "New Troy."

- Before you and a bit to the left are altars and offering shafts dating from Hellenistic Greece. Moving south, we find the Roman gymnasium.

- To the east are more Roman buildings: an odeon with marble seats and a performance area that was once roofed but is now open to the sky. Beyond that is a half-circular building built right against the walls of Troy VI, the council house of the Roman city.

- Between the odeon and the council house is our last main feature of Troy, a Troy VI gate facing south. It has been plausibly argued that this is the Scaean gate, at which Homer set Achilles and Hector's duel.

Istanbul—Capital of the Byzantine Emperors

Lecture 22

I stanbul is one of the world's truly great cities, the largest city in Turkey, and the only important city in the world that straddles two continents—Europe and Asia. It was originally called Byzantion by the Greeks who founded it in 633 B.C. Later called Byzantium by the Romans who made it part of their empire, it became Constantinople when Emperor Constantine the Great moved the capital of the Roman Empire here in the 4th century A.D. It took on its modern name, Istanbul, in the period of the Ottoman domination.

- We will concentrate on the archaeological and historic sites in the old core of the urban center, the little area called Sultanahmet, which includes the site of the original Greek city, the later Roman capital, and the administrative headquarters of the Ottoman Turkish sultans.

- That said, I hope that when you visit, you will not hesitate to move beyond those historic streets and into the drumbeat of modern Turkish life in this bustling and energetic metropolis.

- We are going to take Istanbul in three sections, starting with Byzantine and Roman Istanbul, the city established by Constantine in A.D. 330. Constantine was a remarkable character who became emperor of Rome following a great victory over many rivals.

- According to tradition, one night around the year A.D. 300, Constantine dreamed of his armies going into battle with a Christian emblem on their banners and shields and heard or saw the words *In hoc signo vinces*, "in this sign you will conquer."

- He had not, up to that time, been a Christian, although his mother Helena was, but he had those emblems painted on his armies' shields and banners and won the Battle of the Milvian Bridge, thus becoming the sole ruler of the Roman Empire.

- Shortly thereafter, he decided to move the capital eastward, an extraordinary move. Rome had always been the heart of the empire. But the Western empire was under pressure from barbarians at its borders and from citizens within its provinces. All the wealth and stability seemed to be in the eastern half of the empire.

- Constantine wanted to locate his new capital at Troy, but Byzantium was eventually chosen as the more strategic position. Constantine set up his administrative center right on top of the old Megarian Greek colony, so there is virtually nothing of the Greek city left to look at.

- This is clearly a good spot for a city, on a promontory between the Golden Horn on the north and the Sea of Marmara on the south. Its only defect was a lack of springs, but the Romans were masters of the aqueduct.

- The city's modern name, Istanbul, may be a worn-down version of Constantinopolis, "city of Constantine," or it may come from the Greek phrase *eis ten polein*, "in the city."

- Constantine laid out his forum in an area known today as Çemberlitaş, which lies on the edge of the bazaar district.

- Rising up from the middle of it, 115 feet into the air, is the Column of Constantine. This monument recalls works back in Rome like Trajan's Column but is made of hard, enduring Egyptian porphyry stone. The neighborhood is named for the reinforcing iron hoops that surround the column itself.

- The statue of Constantine as the sun god Helios that once topped the column is missing. Whatever his mother's religion, Constantine seems to have bought into the cult of the Roman emperor. Certainly, he saw his reign as the dawn of a new era for Rome.

- Constantine tackled his city's water problem with a grand aqueduct all the way up the Bosporus, the channel that connects the Black Sea to the Sea of Marmara. The transported water was then stored in gigantic cisterns holding tens of thousands of gallons.

- The cistern was not completed in Constantine's lifetime. Rather, the Emperor Justinian, who also built the Hagia Sophia, completed it. Known as the Basilica Cistern, it is an amazing structure almost as vast as a cathedral lying under the streets of the city.

- To enter the cistern, you enter through a small door and take a long flight of steps downward. Suddenly, from the cavelike darkness, you emerge into a vast chamber of columns, their reflections flickering in the shimmering water, while the sound of dripping condensation echoes all around you.

- The columns are the real attraction here. Twenty-eight rows of 12 columns, each a staggering 40 feet tall, they were brought as spolia from all over Justinian's domain. Where two of them proved to be too short, Justinian's engineers brought in giant Gorgon heads to use as bases—one inverted, one on its side—to lengthen them.

- As you walk through the cistern, a few other remarkable columns capture the attention, including one that seems carved with eyes. These are, in fact, the eyes on peacocks' feathers.

- Spend a little time here to marvel at Roman engineering and respect the way the Romans found such an aesthetically wondrous solution to the practical problem of a water shortage.

- Leaving Constantine's column and the cistern behind us, we come to the southern tip of the promontory on the edge of the Sea of

Marmara. We are looking at the palace district, where Constantine created the equivalent of the Palatine Hill at Rome.

- Constantine took the original agora of the old Greek colony and put a new Christian church on it, which he called the Church of the Holy Wisdom, or Hagia Sophia. (The mosque that stands on that spot today is the third structure to bear the name.)

- Constantine was not a Christian in his lifetime, although he did legalize the practice of Christianity within the empire. The faith was too at odds with the life of a soldier king. However, tradition holds that he converted on his deathbed.

- Constantine's palace adjoined the original Hagia Sophia on one side. Today, that palace is a confused area of tumbled walls and overgrown ruins. I do not recommend trying to explore it yourself, even if you find it open to the public. It is not a particularly secure place to walk around.

- You can see the site's treasures in museums all over Istanbul instead, particularly the Archaeological Museum of Istanbul.

- Also, consider visiting the Great Palace Mosaic Museum. This museum was built right on top of a remarkable, enormous Justinian-era mosaic discovered by accident between the Blue Mosque and Constantine's palace. We do not always think of mosaics as a higher art form, but this mosaic may change your mind.

- From Constantine's palace, there was a covered walkway that connected to the largest single structure in the city, the hippodrome, a track for chariot racing. This was the Circus Maximus of Constantinople.

- If you put together all the enthusiasm for all the sports, films, and other forms of entertainment felt by fans in the modern West today,

I doubt you would even approach the passion that the people of Byzantium came to feel for their hippodrome and the sport of chariot racing.

- The Roman Empire had made chariot racing a team sport. Every charioteer raced under one of four colors: red, white, green, or blue, although little by little in Byzantium, blue and green came to be the only colors.

- Your chariot team affiliation was the equivalent of belonging to a faith or a political party. People got into murderous fights with each other simply because one was blue, one was green.

- The hippodrome is still visible, although its grandstands, which were on two levels, are long gone due to both deliberate destruction and the ravages of time. But you can still see the arcaded curve of fine Byzantine masonry that was the southern terminus of the loop of track.

Emperor Constantine the Great founded Constantinople to be the Rome of the East.

- The open area is today a vast park. Today, this park is where the city of Istanbul celebrates Ramadan, the period of daytime fasting and nighttime feasting that is one of the highlights of the Islamic year.

- The emperors adorned the spina—the central structure that ran down the middle of the hippodrome, around which the chariots would race—with spolia from all over the empire. One is from the oracular shrine at Delphi, a column of three bronze serpents twined around each other. Originally, the three heads looked in three different directions and supported a tripod, although today only one head survives and the tripod is long gone.

- It was cast in bronze in the year 479 B.C. from a tithe (a tenth) of the Persian armor and arms captured by the Greeks in the last great battle of the Persian Wars on Greek territory, the Battle of Plataea. On the lower coil of one of the serpents are the names of the 31 Greek cities and islands that banded together to resist the seemingly invincible army of Xerxes.

- Another of the spolia is a grand Egyptian obelisk—or the upper part of one—from Luxor dating to 1450 B.C. that was originally erected to celebrate the victories of the Pharaoh Thutmose III.

- There's one set of things missing from the spina. When the Venetians captured Constantinople in the Crusade of A.D. 1204, they stole a set of four bronze horses and brought them back to stand in St. Mark's Basilica.

- From the hippodrome, head down toward the water and the Walls of Istanbul, fabulous brick and stone structures that run for 12 miles around the city. These were once the strongest fortifications in the world, supplemented by an immense moat.

- The gates seem to be absolutely unbreakable, and for a millennium those walls held out against all comers. But they are also a sign of something. Cities had no walls in Rome's classical period. Walls are a sign of engineering prowess, but they are also a sign that the empire had become a target.

The Pearl of Constantinople—Hagia Sophia

Lecture 23

D o not be fooled by the rather ordinary exterior of the Hagia Sophia, the church in the heart of Istanbul. After all, if you imagine away the four minarets that were added to transform the church into a mosque and the massive buttresses that were added to stabilize the dome during the Ottoman period, it is a plain building. The dome looks rather low. Other structures seem to huddle around it like chicks around a mother hen. But that plainness is part of the point.

- Classical Greek temples dazzle from the outside because they are meant to be seen from the outside. Only the priest or priestess ever enters to make prayers and offerings to the god or goddess inside.

- At Hagia Sophia, as in all Byzantine churches, the glory is inside because this is a place for an entire community of worshipers to gather, to come from the grim outdoors into this place of light that seemed to mirror a heaven here on earth.

- As you wait in line to enter, take the time to look into some of the trenches near the walls of the modern church. You will see the foundation and a little relief of sheep all in a line on a stone lintel that belonged to the second Hagia Sophia, this church's predecessor.

- The first Hagia Sophia on this site was built by Constantine. It had a wooden roof, and it burned down. Later, Emperor Theodosius built another Hagia Sophia—bigger and grander, to which the stone lintel belonged.

- Theodosius's Hagia Sophia was destroyed in the Nika Riots of A.D. 532, which began in the hippodrome. The riots started in the aftermath of a green-versus-blue chariot race and became a bloody battle that engulfed the city, which was already at the boiling point due to heavy taxes levied by Emperor Justinian.

- Within days of the second church's destruction, Justinian was already planning his new Hagia Sophia, the gigantic church you see before you now.

- He wanted a church that would surpass all others in the audacity of its design. To do that, he sought the best engineers and designers from all over the empire, whether high-born or low. (He was low born himself.)

- Justinian found most of his talent in Turkey, Asia Minor, and Greece. Two men, Isidoros of Miletus and Anthemius of Tralleis, were his chief designers. Although the inspiration for the dome came from Hadrian's Pantheon in Rome, in most respects this building broke new ground.

- Enter the church through the western central door, remembering that we would not have been allowed in this door as ordinary people when Hagia Sophia was built; it was reserved for the emperor and his court.

- Justinian spent as much time thinking about the decorative program for his church as he did about its design. He was inspired in the year A.D. 553 when General Belisarius retrieved the Treasures of Solomon from the Vandal tribes who had looted them from Rome and brought them to Byzantium.

- Justinian was resolved to do two things: to return these treasures to Jerusalem (unfortunately, they would soon disappear beneath the waves of Saracen invaders) and to make his new church as glorious as he imagined the Temple of Solomon had been.

- When entering the church, you might not notice the overall decoration at first because you are struck by the magnificence of what is overhead. First you will see the half-domes of the apses, with their mosaics of Mary holding the infant Jesus.

- Then, as you move further in, you can see above you the full dome at the center of the church, like the opening of heaven itself: 100 feet across, 180 feet high, the height of an 18-story building and seemingly suspended in space.

- How was that done? Justinian's court recorder, a historian named Procopius, gives us a clue and shows us that educated people of that time were just as interested in the engineering behind Hagia Sophia as they were in the emotional effect of all that grandeur:

  > As the four arches are arranged in a square, the stonework connecting them takes the shape of a triangle [what we would call a pendentive]. The lower angle of the triangle is slender, but it widens as it rises into the space between the walls and ends in a circle, which rests upon that. The dome standing on this circle makes it exceedingly beautiful. It does not seem to rest on a solid foundation but seems suspended from heaven by the legendary golden chain.

- Once you can tear your eyes away from the stunning dome, walk around the church and look at the results of Justinian's determination. You will first be struck by the richness of the columns and the fact that they are not all matching. They are spolia.

- In panels on the walls and in inlay on the floor, you will see the glitter of colored stone—purple porphyry from Egypt, green stone from Thessaly, black stone from the Bosporus, yellow stone from Syria, white stone from Cappadocia, golden stone from Libya.

- Look up in the dome again and notice the 40 ribs leading down to a circle of 40 windows. The ribs are hollow tubes of bricks made of porous clay from Rhodes. It is as if each part of Justinian's vast domains contributed something to the building of this remarkable church. This tradition continued on into the Ottoman period.

- Procopius tells us that when Justinian first walked in to the church under the newly finished dome he looked up and said, "Glory to God who considered me worthy to create such a thing. I have surpassed you Solomon."

- Much of the Byzantine furnishing of the church has disappeared, but at the east end there is a square of inlaid marble on the floor called the Omphalion, a term taken from the stone at the Delphic oracular shrine. On that spot stood the throne where each Byzantine emperor after Justinian had his coronation.

- There are also some Islamic features in the church, especially the mimbar, or raised pulpit for preaching, and the mihrab, the prayer niche, which orients the person looking at it in the direction of Mecca.

- The upper galleries are extraordinary places. In Byzantine times, the common people would have more likely attended service in the galleries than in the main body of the church with the emperor and his court.

- The ascent itself is worth contemplating. Instead of a staircase, there is an oblong space full of ramps and switchbacks. According to tradition, this is so that the empress and ladies of the court could be drawn up on sledges, rather than having to walk.

- The first place to visit in the gallery is the West Gallery, where the empress attended services. A circle of green marble marks where her throne once stood. Mosaic portraits of past empresses adorn the walls.

- One particularly interesting mosaic shows the Empress Zoe seated on one side of Jesus. On Jesus's other side is her husband—or rather, all three of her husbands. This mosaic portrait has had three faces over its lifetime. As each husband died, Zoe had the head replaced with the new man's likeness.

- There are graffiti up on this gallery level, carved by the bored and irreverent. One in particular can be found on the south gallery on one of the balustrades where we think the emperor's bodyguards stood. There are a handful of Viking runes; at this time the imperial bodyguards were the Varangian Guard, Swedish Viking mercenaries.

- Among the glories of the galleries are some of the very finest mosaics to be found anywhere on earth, particularly the Deesis mosaic. It shows three figures—Jesus on the cross, flanked by the Virgin Mary and Saint John, set in front of a gold background.

- This mosaic looks different from others in the church. It was a very late addition, dating to the end of the Byzantine Empire. In fact, in the background of the scene, you can see the burial plaque of the doge of Venice, Henricus Dandolo, who had been in charge of the Venetian Conquest of Byzantium in 1204.

- On close examination, the figures have depth and the shadows have direction. After 1453, when Constantinople fell to the Ottoman Turks, the city's artists in many cases fled westward. Some artists from Byzantium ended their days in Italy, and many art historians believe that those who created such masterpieces as the Deesis mosaic helped introduce this same subtlety into the art of the Italian Renaissance.

- Back down on the main level of the church, our ultimate destination is the exit in the southwest corner, through the Warrior's vestibule. As you walk out, look up. You will see a mirror that draws your attention to the mosaic above and behind you.

- This 10th-century mosaic of the Madonna and Child enthroned shows two figures on either side of the Virgin, each offering her something. Constantine offers her the city itself in the form of a small model he holds in his hands. Justinian offers her the Hagia Sophia in its original form—without the minarets and buttresses. We exit the church with a vision of how it was at the beginning.

Ottoman Istanbul—Mosques, Palaces, Bazaars
Lecture 24

To begin this tour of Ottoman Istanbul, let us travel back in time to a most fateful date in human history, May 29, 1453. We stand before Hagia Sophia, and all around us is chaos. The city has been sacked by the army of the Ottoman Turks, led by a 21-year-old conqueror, Mehmet II. As we watch, Mehmet approaches the church and, with great humility, bends to scoop up a handful of dirt and sprinkle it on his head before entering this vast place of worship. From this moment on, Islam, not Christianity will reign in Istanbul.

- Mehmet, dissatisfied with the Byzantine palace, created his own palace for his own dynasty, the Topkapı Palace, "the palace of the gate of the canons" which everyone who visits Turkey should spend a day exploring.

- Around the palace gate, you can see a few of the canons that Mehmet's forces used to conquer the city. This gate was built on the spot where Mehmet built his pavilion and settled in once the city was in his hands.

- In the First Court, or Janissary Court, you would have found right up until 1909 a vast crowd of people, petitioners from all over the empire seeking to address the sultan or one of his ministers.

- Order would be kept among the petitioners by a group of soldiers called Janissaries, clothed in scarlet and accompanied by music. If you are lucky, you will be able to hear the sounds of the modern Janissary Band playing near the Hagia Sophia or even see them on parade.

- Wolfgang Amadeus Mozart and Ludwig van Beethoven both took inspiration from the Janissary Band, Mozart in *The Abduction from the Seraglio* and Beethoven in a section of the "Ode to Joy" in the *Ninth Symphony*.

- In this First Court is a church called Hagia Eirene, one of the very few Byzantine churches that was not converted to a mosque. Instead, it was used as a storage place for the palace.

- The First Court of the palace had a very military look, but once you pass through the gate into the second court, you will find a very different world of trees, lawns, and gardens. The gate itself, on this side, is covered with lovely filigree designs, a thing of grace and beauty rather than military might.

- The Second Court was where the administration of the empire was carried out, especially by the grand vizier and his council.

- You will see on the left the Hall of Justice and the Tower of Justice rising from it, looking very much like the steeple of a Christian church. On your right, you will see a long range of buildings topped with chimneys—the palace kitchens.

- Enter the kitchens and marvel at the number of metal utensils preserved from the time of the sultans—enormous boilers, frying pans, ladles, and spoons. They inspire us to remember that this is a place where one of the world's great cuisines was created.

- Remember also that it was through the sultan's palace at Topkapı that coffee got from the Indian Ocean into the Ottoman Empire and then Europe. In fact, Ottoman envoys to London and Paris would be sent with coffee, knowing the capacity of coffee to loosen tongues and promote gossip.

- You will see in some of the museums in Topkapı some of the most beautiful Chinese and Japanese porcelains in the world. These, too, flowed through Istanbul and through Ottoman ports into European palaces and everyday homes.

- Move on to the grand Third Court and notice the pavilions dotted about. Topkapı was not built to impress visitors as was, say, Versailles or Buckingham Palace. It was built for the pleasure and leisure of its residents as a place where the sultan and his family could be off display.

- We find in this area the treasury and some audience halls, where the sultan used to receive ambassadors from all over the world. These rooms have been transformed into museums and libraries.

- Among the treasures on display are the jeweled and padded divans on which the sultan sat as on a throne when receiving ambassadors and guests. The dagger with three enormous emeralds in the hilt that was the subject of the movie *Topkapi* is also on display.

- You will also see remarkable relics, such as a letter possibly written by Mohammed the Prophet himself, found in Egypt, and a skull purported to belong to John the Baptist.

- In the library is a fabulous map created by an Ottoman mapmaker and geographer named Piri Reis who lived in Gallipoli in the 16th century. It contains representations of the coastlines of Europe, Africa, and South America so precise you can pick out individual river mouths.

- In the Fourth Court, you will find an open terrace, placed today in the room where sons of the Ottoman sultans received their circumcisions, an important rite of passage in Turkish culture even today.

- Tulip festivals also took place in this courtyard. The Turks love tulips more than any other flower. On the day in spring when the tulips were at their height, the women from the harem, perhaps a thousand of them, would be allowed to come out for one evening into these gardens to take in the views of the flowers and the stars.

- A separate part of the Topkapı Palace very rarely visited is the harem, or hareem, itself. This "forbidden place," the palace of women, has been running alongside on your left as you have made your way through the Second and Third Courts.

- It contains 300 rooms and once held a thousand concubines. There are throne rooms, kitchens, doctors' quarters, pavilions, music rooms, baths, all beautifully preserved. You will need a separate ticket to enter.

- Now it is time to leave the palace and visit two places along the hippodrome that have Ottoman connections: a museum and a mosque.

- The Museum of Turkish and Islamic Arts includes the greatest collection of carpets in the world. Many tourists visiting Turkey come home with one or more carpets; it is a good idea to visit the museum if only to have a standard to compare the bazaar's wares to. The museum's café also has a porch with a great view of the hippodrome and authentic Turkish coffee.

- The Blue Mosque is one of the most beautiful religious buildings in the world. It sits in the Sultanahmet region of Istanbul, named for 17th-century ruler Sultan Ahmed I, who wanted to build this mosque to rival Hagia Sophia.

- Ahmed's architect undertook to create a dome that in beauty, if not in height, would certainly shine alongside the great dome of Justinian. The building has six minarets, which was shocking at the time because only the mosque of the Ka'bah in Mecca was supposed to have six minarets. Beneath the minarets lies a forest of silvery domes and half-domes.

- Muslims who intend to pray at the mosque may enter through the Grand Courtyard, a colonnaded court that echoes the courtyard that used to stand outside Hagia Sophia. Others should go around to the north side to the visitors' entrance.

- Non-Muslim visitors unfamiliar with mosque etiquette should also note, you will be asked to exchange your street shoes for slippers, and women must cover their heads and limbs. While there is no entrance fee, consider making a donation toward the running of these visitors' services.

The Blue Mosque is less well known than the Hagia Sophia and offers the visitor a very different but no less remarkable experience.

- Upon entering, you will experience something very different from what you felt in Hagia Sophia. It is so gleaming and perfect, it seems as if it were finished yesterday and not back in the 1600s.

- The dome is supported by four giant columns, like the legs of an elephant, which creates a very different feel from that open, suspended feeling of Hagia Sophia, more a feeling of massive strength underlying the delicate beauty.

- The mimbar is reached by a white marble staircase. Hanging from the ceiling are immense chandeliers. This a complicated place, and yet a place of transporting beauty, even for those who come to gaze rather than to pray.

- As we move toward the end of our Ottoman tour, we return to the Column of Constantine and Çemberlitaş. There is also a great Islamic monument here, opposite the column: the Çemberlitaş Hamam, or bath, by Islam's greatest architect, Sinan.

- *Hamams* were an essential element of Islamic culture, used for ritual bathing and purification. Most big mosques would have a *hamam* attached so people could clean themselves before they went in to pray. Think how different this was from Europe in the Middle Ages and the Renaissance, when people might bathe as little as once a year.

- Today, men and women alike can enter Sinan's beautiful Çemberlitaş Hamam. Men may visit the steam room and lie seminaked on slabs of warm marble under the great dome. If you wish, you may pay extra to receive a massage, but note that this *hamam* is frequented by tourists and is not the best bargain spa in the city.

- Very near the *hamam* is the entrance to the Grand Bazaar. Please do not disdain it. It is huge and historic, covering many city blocks and filled with everything you can imagine among a confusing melee of lights and glittering storefronts.

- Right in the center is an area built by Mehmet II to start the business of import and export in the heart of his new capital city.

- We are going to end our day with a boat ride. Take a taxi to the Bosporus waterfront for a moonlit ride on a rented ferry or sailboat. Look back at all the wonderful sites you have seen these past few days.

- I recommend landing for supper at a place called Ortaköy, an ordinary neighborhood with a 19th-century mosque, small streets, and very friendly people, where you can enjoy an evening among the ordinary life of this extraordinary city.

- This is a particularly good spot to do so because, from these outdoor cafés, you can see the Bosporus I Bridge, an enormous suspension bridge that in the late 20th century finally linked Europe and Asia across the rushing waters of the Bosporus.

- For millennia, many people believed the differences between Europe and Asia, West and East, are irreconcilable on political, religious, and cultural levels. Here in Istanbul is a city that spans the divide.

- This bridge is the ultimate symbol that this is not a broken world, divided across a fault line, but a world united by the great works of humans throughout history.

Map of Athens and the Acropolis

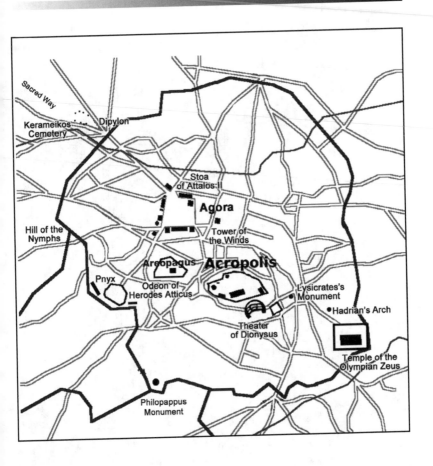

Map of Istanbul

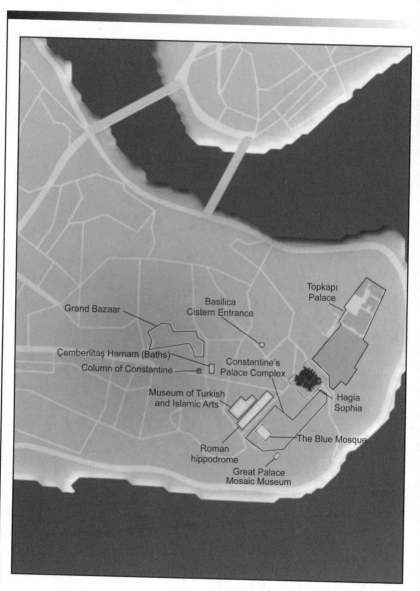

Embassy Contact Information

Note: If your nation's embassies are not listed here, we strongly recommend you find the information and carry it with you when you travel.

Greece

Australian Embassy
Level 6, Thon Building
Kifisias & Alexandras Avenues
Ambelokipi
115 23 Athens
Phone: 30-210-870-4000
Fax: 30-210-870-4111
E-mail: ae.athens@dfat.gov.au

British Embassy
1 Ploutarchou Street
106 75 Athens, Greece
Phone: 30-210-727-2600
Fax: 30-210-727-2743
E-mail: consular.athens@fco.gov.uk

Canadian Embassy
4 Ioannou Gennadiou Street
115 21 Athens, Greece
Phone: 30-210-727-3400
Fax: 30-210-727-3480
E-mail: athns@international.gc.ca

United States Embassy
91 Vasilisis Sophias Avenue
10160 Athens, Greece
Phone: 30-210-721-2951
E-mail: AthensAmEmb@state.gov

Turkey

Australian Embassy
MNG Building
Ugur Mumcu Caddesi No: 88, 7th Floor
Gaziosmanpasa 06700, Ankara
Phone: 90-312-459-9500
Fax: 90-312-446-4827
E-mail: consular.ankara@dfat.gov.au

British Embassy
Şehit Ersan Caddesi 46/A
Çankaya
Phone: 90-312-455-3344
Fax: 90-312-455-3352

Canadian Embassy
Cinnah Caddesi no: 58
06690 Cankaya
Ankara
Phone: 90-312-409-2700
Fax: 90-312-409-2712
E-mail: ankra@international.gc.ca

United States Embassy
110 Atatürk Boulevard
Kavaklidere
06100 Ankara
Phone: 90-312-455-5555
Fax: 90-312-467-0019
E-mail: webmaster_ankara@state.gov

Contact Information for Major Sites

Most of the major sites of Greece are administered by the Hellenic Ministry of Culture and Tourism. Their website (http://odysseus.culture.gr/index_en.html) should be your first stop when looking for a phone number or hours of operation for museums, monuments, historical sites, and archaeological digs anywhere in Greece, including the island of Crete. Sites of particular prominence or those not operated by the ministry are listed separately below.

The Acropolis Museum
http://www.theacropolismuseum.gr

Archaeological Work at the Athens Metro (AttikoMetro)
http://www.ametro.gr/page/default.asp?la=2&id=13

The Corinth Canal
http://www.periandros.gr/

The National Archaeological Museum of Greece
http://www.namuseum.gr/wellcome-en.html

Similarly, the Republic of Turkey Ministry of Culture and Tourism maintains a central website (http://www.kultur.gov.tr/EN/) that serves as a clearinghouse of information for the nation's national museums, monuments, and archaeological sites. Some subsites and external sites of particular interest are as follows.

Hagia Sophia
http://www.kultur.gov.tr/EN/belge/2-19960/istanbul---hagia-sophia-museum.html

Topkapı Palace Museum
http://www.kultur.gov.tr///-19974/--topkapi-palace-museum.html

Natural and Cultural Properties on the World Heritage List in Turkey
http://www.kultur.gov.tr///-20211/on-the-world-heritage-list.html

Bibliography

Note: Modern travelers to Greece and Turkey can choose from a wide range of illustrated guidebooks that include maps, site plans, remarkable photographs, and practical information to whet the appetite. In addition, in both Greece and Turkey you can buy excellent guides to specific sites and museums, rich in photographs and historical background, with texts by Greek or Turkish archaeologists who can speak with authority about the monuments and other discoveries. Both types of book are updated almost annually, so editions come and go rapidly. By all means, invest in these books. The bibliography presented here, however, concentrates on literary works that will provide invaluable background information—as well as inspiration—as you plan your own itinerary and prepare for your own adventures.

Allen, Susan Heuck. *Finding the Walls of Troy: Frank Calvert and Heinrich Schliemann at Hisarlik*. Berkeley: University of California Press, 1999. The most authoritative study yet written on the discovery of Troy, the truth concerning Schliemann's motives and accomplishments, and their impact on classical archaeology and the world at large.

Amandry, Pierre. *Delphi and Its History*. Athens: Archaeological Guide Editions, 1984. French archaeologist Amandry has devoted his career to the study of the Delphic Oracle site, and his authoritative essays are here illustrated with excellent maps, drawings, and photographs.

Barret, André. *Greece Observed*. New York: Oxford University Press, 1974. The book is notable for its excellent aerial photographs, but Barret's text also provides an outstanding introduction to the sites and their geographical settings.

Bowden, Hugh. *Mystery Cults of the Ancient World*. Princeton, NJ: Princeton University Press, 2010. This sumptuously presented and illustrated tome has an authoritative text on the history, beliefs, and practices of the various cults, along with fine photographs of sites and artifacts. Among the cults covered are the Eleusinian Mysteries, the cult of the Great Mother of the Gods (Asiatic Cybele), Dionysus, Isis, and Mithras.

Bradford, Ernle. *The Companion Guide to the Greek Islands*. 6th ed. Woodbridge, UK: Companion Guides, 1998. Unlike Lawrence Durrell (see below), Bradford provides a systematic tour of all the Greek islands, including geographical and historical sketches; information on monuments, landscapes, and local life; and even recommendations for the best beaches.

Camp, John M. *The Archaeology of Athens*. New Haven, CT: Yale University Press, 2004. All of Athens and Attica is included in this handsomely illustrated volume, written by the famous American archaeologist who directs excavations at the Athenian Agora.

Casson, Lionel. *Travel in the Ancient World*. Baltimore, MD: Johns Hopkins University Press, 1994. The author, an authority on ancient seafaring, writes about the experiences of ancient Greek and Roman travelers in a way that is both erudite and entertaining.

Cimok, Fatih. *A Guide to the Seven Churches*. Istanbul: A Turizim Yaryimlan Publication, 1998. Turkish scholar Cimok has written an excellent guide to the seven churches of Asia mentioned by Saint John in the book of Revelation, including such important sites as Pergamum, Ephesus, Smyrna (modern Izmir), and Sardis. There is also a preliminary chapter on the island of Patmos. Excellent plans and photos illustrate the text.

Connolly, Peter, and Andrew Solway. *Ancient Greece*. Oxford: Oxford University Press, 2001. Connolly is the most respected living illustrator of classical civilizations, bringing the past to life with painstakingly accurate yet extremely lively color paintings of ancient cities and monuments and the people who built and used them. This book is a great help in reconstructing in the mind's eye the full splendor of buildings that now survive only in fragments.

Curnow, Trevor. *The Oracles of the Ancient World: A Comprehensive Guide*. London: Duckworth, 2004. This detailed survey of classical oracles, country by country and site by site, lays particular emphasis on sanctuaries in Greece and Turkey and is written by a scholar whose descriptions are derived from personal travels to these important sacred places.

Dankoff, Robert, and Sooyong Kim, trans. and eds. *An Ottoman Traveller: Selections from the Book of Travels of Evliya Celebi*. London: Eland Books, 2011. This new translation of the most captivating passages from Evliya Celebi's 10-volume compendium allows the modern visitor to Turkey to see the land through the lens of the 17th century, when the Ottoman Empire reached its zenith.

De Jongh, Brian. *The Companion Guide to Mainland Greece*. Rev. ed. London: HarperCollins, 1989. Concise yet comprehensive, this book provides the traveler with a reliable guide to hundreds of sites and suggests itineraries in various regions of Greece that will link nearby sites into an exciting and illuminating tour.

Durrell, Lawrence. *The Greek Islands*. London: Faber and Faber, 2002. This beautifully written and illustrated book is a true classic in the genre of travel writing. Durrell has written not a systematic guidebook but a series of very personal essays, almost like letters home, in which he meditates on his voyages through the seas around Greece, the special spirit of each island, and the people he met along the way.

Fant, Clyde and Mitchell Reddish. *A Guide to Biblical Sites in Greece and Turkey*. New York: Oxford University Press, 2003. The authors are experienced travelers who provide detailed site tours, with an emphasis on ancient cities visited by the Apostle Paul. Old Testament sites in eastern Turkey, such as Mount Ararat, are not included.

Freely, John. *Strolling through Athens*. New York: Tauris Park Paperbacks, 2004. Freely proves to be the ideal walking companion for this stroll through the historic center of Greece's capital, very much in the spirit of the words of Cicero (written in 79 B.C.) that open Freely's book: "There is no end to it in this city. Wherever we walk, we set foot upon some history."

———. *The Western Shores of Turkey: Discovering the Aegean and Mediterranean Coasts*. London: Tauris Parke Paperbacks, 2004. One of the most respected of modern travel essayists turns his attention to western Turkey and evokes both past glories and present beauties for the prospective visitor.

154

Horwitz, Sylvia. *The Find of a Lifetime: Sir Arthur Evans and the Discovery of Knossos*. New York: Viking Press, 1981. Anyone planning a visit to the Palace of Knossos near Heraklion in Crete should first read this dramatic retelling of the excavations that brought it to light, along with a fascinating portrait of its discoverer.

Lloyd, Seton. *Ancient Turkey: A Traveller's History*. Berkeley: University of California Press, 1999. The author, an archaeologist with wide experience in the Near East, provides an overview of Turkey's ancient wonders, striking a fine balance between historical sketches of ancient civilizations (Neolithic, Hittite, Lycian, and many others) and excellent tours of specific sites.

Pamuk, Orhan. *Istanbul: Memories and the City*. New York: Vintage, 2006. Turkey's first winner of the Nobel Prize for Literature has created a dual portrait of his family and of his city that is strongly felt, deeply melancholy, and endlessly fascinating.

Parlama, Liana. *Athens: The City beneath the City—Antiquities from the Metropolitan Railway Excavations*. New York: Harry N. Abrams, 2000. Do not be fooled by the coffee table appearance of this lavishly illustrated volume. It is a detailed and absorbing guide to the spectacular discoveries made in recent years in downtown Athens. Many of the artifacts are now displayed in the metro stations themselves.

Pausanias. *Guide to Greece*. 2 vols. Harmondsworth, UK: Penguin Classics, 1984. A modern English translation of the oldest surviving guidebook, written by a Greek traveler and scholar in the 2nd century A.D. and intended for the use of wealthy Greek and Roman tourists. Pausanias covers mainland Greece south of Thermopylae and retails the patter of local guides and priests along with many myths and historical anecdotes. Long on monuments, short on landscapes.

Plimer, Ian. *Milos: Geologic History*. Athens: Koan Publishers, 2000. If a more beautiful book exists, I have yet to see it. Plimer has written an evocative and poetic text that is nonetheless packed with practical information about the geology and landscapes of Milos, but the matchless photographs raise this book to another level altogether.

Spawforth, Tony. *The Complete Greek Temples*. London: Thames & Hudson, 2006. Spawforth has created an indispensable and beautifully illustrated reference work that breathes new life into the ruined remains of temples throughout Greece and the Aegean.

Stafford-Deitsch, Jeremy. *Kingdom of Ruins: The Art and Architectural Splendors of Ancient Turkey*. London: I. B. Tauris, 2010. This rich collection of extraordinary photographs and evocative descriptions covers civilizations from the Stone Age to the Classical period.

Stoneman, Richard, ed. *A Literary Companion to Travel in Greece*. Malibu, CA: J. Paul Getty Museum, 1994. This handsomely illustrated volume includes excerpts from both ancient and modern writers who were inspired by Greek landscapes and monuments. The book is arranged topographically for easy reference to specific sites and itineraries.

Streeter, Michael. *The Mediterranean: Cradle of European Culture*. London: New Holland Publishers, 2006. The magnificent photographs in this volume accompany a fast-paced but lucid survey of the Mediterranean world, ranging from chapters on the natural setting and the Stone Age up to the Byzantine and Ottoman empires.

Talbert, Richard. *Barrington Atlas of the Greek and Roman World*. Princeton, NJ: Princeton University Press, 2000. This monument of scholarship and cartography includes magnificent topographic maps (as well as detailed maps of ancient cities) in Greece, Turkey, and beyond. Huge, costly, but indispensable. The book comes with a supplementary CD-ROM with additional data.

Taplin, Oliver. *Greek Fire: The Influence of Ancient Greece on the Modern World*. New York: Atheneum Press, 1990. This brilliant survey of cultural heritage brings the ancient world to life by examining, in the liveliest possible fashion, its influence on contemporary politics, theater, sexual mores, art, architecture, and daily life. Excellent and often surprising illustrations accompany Taplin's lively writing.

Tsigakou, Fani-Maria. *The Rediscovery of Greece: Travellers and Painters of the Romantic Era*. London: Thames & Hudson, 1981. After a brilliantly written and illustrated survey of the early forays made by Europeans into Byzantine and Ottoman Greece, Tsikagou presents a stimulating review of the century from 1790 to 1890 and introduces the reader to many Europeans such as Lord Byron who found inspiration for art and literature in their journeys through Greece.

Valavanis, Panos. *Games and Sanctuaries in Ancient Greece: Olympia, Delphi, Isthmia, Nemea, Athens*. Los Angeles, CA: J. Paul Getty Trust, 2004. This big book covers an epic subject, with focus on the archaeological clues that allow us to reconstruct ancient athletic contests, along with the monuments that commemorated great champions, the layouts of the stadiums, and the religious dimension of the ancient games.

Vasilakis, Antonis. *The 147 Cities of Ancient Crete*. Herakleion, Crete: Kairatos Editions, 2000. This is a truly comprehensive historical tour of ancient sites on Crete, with site maps and color photographs of important artifacts. The author includes directions to help locate some of the more obscure sites.

Warren, Peter. *The Aegean Civilizations*. New York: Peter Bedrick Books, 1989. This slim volume packs a terrific punch, covering the origins of the Aegean Sea and its islands, the appearance of Neolithic communities in the archipelagos, the Cycladic civilization with its extraordinary white marble figurines and statues, the destruction of Akrotiri on Thera, the Minoan palaces of Crete, and the appearance of Mycenaeans, leading to the cultural catastrophe at the end of the Bronze Age.

Wheeler, Mortimer, ed. *Swans Hellenic Cruises: Handbook for 1962 Cruises*. London: W. F. and R. K. Swan, 1962. This hard-to-find volume is worth its weight in gold. It carries us back to the glory days of travel through Greece and Turkey, when Swan Tours hired an all-star team of scholars to write essays on the sites that lay along the cruise itinerary. Most of the sites covered in this course are included. Introductory essays cover topics such as Greek and Turkish wines, wildflowers, mythology, architecture, and chronology.

Woods, Michael. *In Search of the Trojan War*. Berkeley: University of California Press, 1998. This popular best seller offers an excellent introduction to the many questions raised by excavations at Troy (Hisarlik) and what the discoveries may tell us about the historical reality behind Homer's epic poem the *Iliad*.

Notes

Notes